STUDENT LEARNING COMMUNITIES

ASCD MEMBER BOOK

Many ASCD members received this book as a
member benefit upon its initial release.

Learn more at: **www.ascd.org/memberbooks**

DOUGLAS FISHER   NANCY FREY   JOHN ALMARODE

STUDENT LEARNING COMMUNITIES

A Springboard for Academic and
Social-Emotional Development

 Alexandria, Virginia USA

1703 N. Beauregard St. • Alexandria, VA 22311-1714 USA
Phone: 800-933-2723 or 703-578-9600 • Fax: 703-575-5400
Website: www.ascd.org • E-mail: member@ascd.org
Author guidelines: www.ascd.org/write

Ranjit Sidhu, *CEO & Executive Director;* Stefani Roth, *Publisher;* Genny Ostertag, *Director, Content Acquisitions;* Julie Houtz, *Director, Book Editing & Production;* Katie Martin, *Editor;* Thomas Lytle, *Creative Director;* Donald Ely, *Art Director;* Keith Demmons, *Senior Production Designer;* Kelly Marshall, *Manager, Project Management;* Shajuan Martin, *E-Publishing Specialist*

PAPERBACK ISBN: 978-1-4166-2965-8   ASCD product #121030
PDF E-BOOK ISBN: 978-1-4166-2966-5; see Books in Print for other formats.
Quantity discounts are available: e-mail programteam@ascd.org or call 800-933-2723, ext. 5773, or 703-575-5773. For desk copies, go to www.ascd.org/deskcopy.

ASCD Member Book No. FY21-2 (Nov. 2020 PSI+). ASCD Member Books mail to Premium (P), Select (S), and Institutional Plus (I+) members on this schedule: Jan, PSI+; Feb, P; Apr, PSI+; May, P; Jul, PSI+; Aug, P; Sep, PSI+; Nov, PSI+; Dec, P. For current details on membership, see www.ascd.org/membership.

Library of Congress Cataloging-in-Publication Data
Names: Fisher, Douglas, 1965- author. | Frey, Nancy, 1959- author. |
    Almarode, John, author.
Title: Student learning communities : a springboard for academic and
    social-emotional development / Douglas Fisher, Nancy Frey, John
    Almarode.
Description: Alexandria, Va. : ASCD, 2021. | Includes bibliographical
    references and index.
Identifiers: LCCN 2020034515 (print) | LCCN 2020034516 (ebook) | ISBN
    9781416629658 (paperback) | ISBN 9781416629665 (pdf)
Subjects: LCSH: Student learning communities. | Academic achievement. |
    Affective education.
Classification: LCC LB1032 .F47 2021 (print) | LCC LB1032 (ebook) | DDC
    371.26--dc23
LC record available at https://lccn.loc.gov/2020034515
LC ebook record available at https://lccn.loc.gov/2020034516

30 29 28 27 26 25 24 23 22 21   1 2 3 4 5 6 7 8 9 10 11 12

STUDENT LEARNING COMMUNITIES

A Springboard for Academic and Social-Emotional Development

Why Student Learning Communities Matter

What teacher hasn't experienced group work gone bad?

We all know that we're supposed to have students collaborate with one another, but this practice is so often fraught with problems. One student does all of the work while others observe or, worse, disengage. Groups divide and conquer the task, and members don't ever interact with one another. Students talk about whatever they want when the teacher is not nearby and, consequently, do not finish the task. What starts as fun interaction devolves into a chaotic carnival disconnected from learning objectives. The task is so easy, or so difficult, that students are so bored or so frustrated that they simply don't do it. Every one of these situations may be familiar to you from past efforts to create opportunities for students to learn with and from one another. And if you've ever designed a group project gone awry, you're probably nodding in agreement right now.

Yes, the promise of student-to-student collaboration is often at odds with what actually goes on in our classrooms. Maybe the following experience, described by mathematics teacher Grace Coates (2005), is familiar to you as well?

> Where I had imagined cooperative dialogue, there was bickering and arguing over materials. Where I had envisioned smiles, many students wore sullen looks. A few wore triumphant smiles as they managed to take over the work or materials. Where I had hoped for thoughtful curiosity,

there were pleading looks saying, "What do I do?" I was so disappointed by these results and my inability to change things in a way that would get my students working productively. (p. 11)

What was missing in Coates's classroom, and what is often missing in group work, are not just the principles that build community and preserve focus but also the skills that allow students to benefit from the experience. Coates admits that she originally believed just putting students in groups would result in better learning. She came to realize more was required. Her students needed to learn how to communicate with one another over a meaningful task. They needed to know what success looked like and how to support each other in the pursuit and attainment of that success.

Instead of assuming that the group work students are doing is good enough, instead of hoping that collaboration will be its own reward, and instead of holding our breath every time group work starts in the hope that it will be productive, what if teachers structured that work more intentionally and purposefully? What if we equipped students with the skills and conditions they need to learn in a way that is truly collective and does make them "smarter together" than they would be as individuals?

The learning process requires the active involvement of the learner (Bransford, Brown, & Cocking, 2000). Decades ago, education was largely focused on acquisition of knowledge, with little consideration given to what went on in the minds of learners. The cognitive sciences and the emergence of awareness of *metacognition* (thinking about one's thinking) have since helped teachers divine how students are processing and manipulating information. Increasingly, our aim is not for students to simply recall and recognize information; these are entry points, not destinations. Our goals for students, the destinations we set and endeavor to help them reach, include cognitive learning outcomes, conceptual understanding, creative problem solving, the development of communication skills, and social-emotional outcomes. In the end, *outcomes* today are measured in terms of transfer of learning—that is, the ability to apply knowledge in new situations to meet new challenges (Bransford et al., 2000).

Student learning communities (SLCs) are a way to recalibrate "group work" to transcend the format's traditional limitations and pursue these essential modern outcomes. It's a model dependent on the active involvement of each member of a learning team and designed to combine the skills and insights of each member in a way that allows all members to learn deeply and collectively.

In the spring of 2020, when distance learning came to dominate teachers' lives, many of us became newly cognizant of just how important it is for students to learn with and from one another. Yes, collaboration had long been identified as a "21st century learning skill" necessary for "the workforce of the future"; two decades into the century, it seems the future really has arrived. It means working from home instead of classrooms and offices. It means connecting with, solving problems with, and learning from others virtually instead of in person. We have also seen how the physical separation of students from their peers leaves many feeling isolated. We have recognized the toll it takes

> As an accompaniment to this book, we have created an additional resource designed to further deep collective learning in virtual environments. It is available as a free download at www. ascd.org/ASCD/pdf/ books/SLCVirtual.

on them (and on us, their teachers). As a result, we believe it is crucial to prioritize ways for students to interact meaningfully in virtual environments in order to mitigate some of these effects. And while the setting may be different in a physically distanced classroom space or an online learning platform, the principles of how people learn together are the same.

The Principles of Learning Communities

The idea of collective learning—of leveraging collective wisdom to promote the growth of the group *as* a group *and* as individuals—is not new to teachers. It's perhaps most familiar as the aim of professional learning communities (PLCs), educator networks that emerged as a response to the often-isolated nature of classroom teaching. We recognized there was an urgent problem with "business as usual" in schools: closed classroom doors that left many practitioners teaching inside of a bubble . . . each of us left to our own devices to design, develop, and implement instruction and interpret assessment results. Why would teachers, as professionals, not want to pool our collective expertise and work collaboratively to advance our skills and improve our students' learning?

The PLC approach also acknowledges, and is guided by, another reality: teachers are not sitting around with an abundance of spare time. We need assurance that the hours devoted to interacting with peers are worthwhile— that they are an investment that will yield tangible benefits for ourselves, our colleagues, and our students.

Accordingly, successful PLCs, like all successful collaborative learning arrangements, are guided by a collective agreement to pursue useful goals in an organized way. This helps avoid the problem of "collaboration for the sake of collaboration" and keeps the work focused. In other words, just because there's a round table doesn't make the people sitting there a learning community. Certain conditions must be present. Over the years, educators have learned that

- PLCs are a way to connect teachers with purpose and success—a way to acquire and hone skills and achieve meaningful and rewarding outcomes.
- PLCs activate collective skills and wisdom, and they are characterized by structures that allow teachers to help one another develop expertise and abilities.

What does it take to transform a group of individuals into a learning community? When Shirley Hord (2004) explored the conditions that facilitate collaborative learning in PLCs composed of teacher teams, she identified six critical factors:

1. Structural conditions that provide a framework for collaboration and the resources to engage in the collaborative work;

2. The fostering, nurturing, and sustaining of productive and professional relationships among members of the collaborative team;

3. The existence of shared values and purpose that motivate individual members to invest in the work of the collaborative team;

4. The intentional leveraging of the collective expertise;

5. All members working to enhance one another's individual efficacy and credibility; and

6. All members leveraging their individual strengths to share leadership responsibilities.

The six elements that make collaborative learning transformative for teams of teachers—the components that transform them from "a group of people working together" into "a learning community"—have the potential to do the same for groups of students.

Think of your own practice, your own students. As you strive to have them engage one another in their learning, you must ensure that they have the skills and dispositions to be successful. This requires you to approach collective learning through the natural progression of gradually releasing responsibility for the work to them. For example, if your learners are to foster shared agreements of success among members of their group, you must first model and engage them in the processes of goal setting, linking individual goals to group goals, and progress monitoring. If your learners are to leverage the support of their peers to amplify learning, you must first model and engage them in effective feedback. It's through this intentional design and implementation of collaborative learning that any teacher can set the stage for learners to engage in SLCs.

Consider what makes for a successful professional learning community—the combination of structures, objectives, priorities, and operations. As illustrated in Figure 1.1, there is considerable overlap between what a PLC needs to function well and the conditions that allow for the kind of deep collective classroom-based learning pursued in student learning communities. Just like a PLC, if an SLC is to thrive, it must engage in a cycle of inquiry. And as in a PLC, sustaining this cycle of inquiry requires SLC members to develop the skills and dispositions necessary to take an active role in their own learning process. For that, they need their teacher's guidance and support.

FIGURE 1.1

The Parallel Conditions for Successful PLCs and SLCs

PLCs need	SLCs need
Structural conditions that provide a framework for collaboration and the resources to engage in the collaborative work	Experiences and tasks that encourage student dialogue
Relationships among team members that are respectful, nurturing, and productive	Supportive relational conditions that empower learning
Shared values and purpose that motivate individual members to invest in the work of the team	Shared agreements about success
Intentional collective learning that builds skills, expertise, and efficacy	Intentional collective learning that builds cognitive and metacognitive skills
Intentional leveraging of staff supports to enhance overall efficacy	Intentional leveraging of peer supports that amplify learning
Intentional work to capitalize on each member's strengths and share leadership responsibilities	The activation of leadership skills students need to succeed—alone and together

Student Learning Communities as the Means to Improve Student Learning

Fortunately, the majority of teachers who have seen collaborative learning flop in the classroom have also seen it succeed. We have witnessed students working together in ways that meet the "learning community" standard, leveraging their collective knowledge, skills, and understandings and consolidating what they know and can do to go further and deeper together than they could have alone.

Consider the example of students in a 5th grade social studies class studying traditional Native American societies and foodways. One of the collaborative learning tasks involved researching food sources and the influence of geography on supply. Each group of learners had a different food source to investigate, and each member of the group had to locate information to share with the group. Each learner had access to digital and print resources, and part of their individual task was to evaluate the credibility of each resource (and some were questionable). Then, as a group, they worked to reach consensus about the information to share out with the rest of class. Each member presented his or her findings, then together they generated a group summary of their assigned food source. Here's an excerpted paragraph from the composition written by the "acorns" group:

> Collecting acorns is a complicated task. You need to be able to identify the good from the bad. When you look for acorns in the fall, when they are ripe, they may fall to the ground. When you start to collect them, be sure to collect the ones *with* their "caps." If you collect the ones without caps, they might have insect larvae inside. This is mainly because an acorn without a cap has probably fallen due to the worm's activity in the acorn, causing it to shake loose of the cap. You also have to look carefully at the ones you collect for holes in the acorn's shell, as these will also indicate the presence of a foul acorn.

When asked about their processes, the students explained that one member's contribution shaped the whole group's thinking. "Jonathan was telling us about what he had found out about poisonous plants in his scout troop, and it got all of us thinking about what could be dangerous in the food supply," said Claire. "That's what changed our investigation," added Spencer.

The paragraph they wrote makes sense and conveys accurate and interesting information. But, more important, it illustrates how these learners moved beyond being just another group of students working together on a project—gathering information, consolidating it, presenting it, checking off the steps to task completion. It's a representation of the everyday transformational work of a community of learners, sparked by the new information and perspective introduced by one of its members.

There are also other elements that mark this collaboration as student learning rather than just a group of students working together. The members of the group demonstrated a social sensitivity and willingness to entertain Jonathan's somewhat tangential knowledge. They had to make some rapid decisions about whether the possible shift in direction would be consistent with their shared agreement of success. At some point, leaders emerged from within this community to allocate resources in order to bring the task to completion. Pretty impressive for 10-year-olds. And yet, you can likely identify many similar examples from your own students, not every time they work in groups, perhaps, but at least often enough for you to see what group learning could be, and at least often enough that you keep chasing those outcomes with new group assignments.

The point is, we know student collaboration can be a springboard to better learning—not just academic learning, but social and emotional learning too. And while this exchange took place in a face-to-face classroom, it just as easily could have occurred in a virtual one, with the addition of some collaborative tools allowing students to talk to and write with one another. How can we ensure this happens reliably for all of our students, rather than just some of the time for some of our students? By attending to the six elements that transform a group of students into a student learning community.

An SLC is achieved by design and through effort, not by luck. In order for students to engage in the collaborative learning process (see Figure 1.2), we, their teachers, need to provide them with the necessary conditions, tools, and supports. That means

- Designing **experiences and tasks** that invigorate learning through academic discourse;
- Attending to **academic, social, and emotional learning**;
- Fostering **shared agreements of individual and group success**;
- Using thoughtful teaming practices to build **cognitive, metacognitive, and emotional regulation** skills;
- Leveraging **peer supports** to amplify learning; and
- Activating all students' **leadership skills** in order to enhance their ability to succeed—alone *and* together.

FIGURE 1.2
The Process of Learning in Student Learning Communities

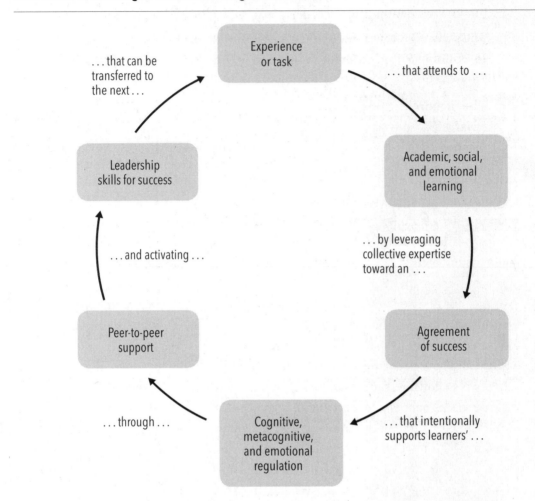

Now, what we intend to do collaboratively with you in the pages ahead is explore each of the six conditions necessary for successful SLCs—which also happen to be the six conditions necessary for effective collaborative learning. It's essential to understand these conditions in order to create them, and a key understanding is that creating them is not a one-time thing. For students to develop and strengthen the skills they need to engage in deep collective learning, they need teachers to model these skills and provide ongoing support.

In sum, this book offers an in-depth look at how to maximize students' academic, social, and emotional development through the practice of student learning communities. There are three takeaways that will unfold in the chapters ahead:

1. **SLCs are more than just a different way of doing group work.** They are a means to foster and sustain students' ability to take ownership of their own learning.

2. **SLCs require teachers to be intentional about engaging students in collaboration.** Knowing when to employ this approach is part of knowing how to employ it.

3. **The academic, social, and emotional skills necessary for successful SLCs must be taught,** ideally through the gradual release of responsibility framework. This ultimately enhances collective learning by leveraging the collective efficacy of the community.

Moving Forward . . .

As teachers, we know our purpose. We want our students to be meet specific milestones, and we want them to become better learners. We want to help them achieve cognitive learning outcomes, develop conceptual understanding, solve problems creatively, and communicate effectively. Research confirms that well-planned collaborative learning experiences can achieve these goals (Cohen & Lotan, 2014). When the elements that make collaborative learning transformative are present in our classrooms, be they "brick" or "click," we see the improved social and emotional learning outcomes, as well as improved behavioral engagement (Johnson & Johnson, 2009). Finally, leveraging the collective wisdom of all learners means embracing diversity; in that way, SLCs are another pathway for ensuring equity of access and opportunity for all learners.

Let's get started!

Tasks and Experiences That Encourage Student Dialogue

"The way to get a good idea is to get lots of ideas."

This insight is widely attributed to the Nobel Prize–winning chemist and peace activist Linus Pauling, the only man to have won a Nobel in two different fields. Pauling's achievement might have been singular, but his work was collaborative, hinging on the free exchange of ideas at his lab at Caltech as he and his colleagues worked out the problem of electronegativity and its relationship to ionic bonds between atoms.

You may not be running a quantum chemistry research lab, but, like Pauling, you are in the business of fostering the generation of ideas that lead to learning. Doing this successfully requires you to attend to the first necessary condition for establishing and sustaining a student learning community (SLC): providing well-designed experiences and tasks that incorporate and encourage student dialogue.

Recall from Chapter 1 the experience of mathematics teacher Grace Coates (2005), who naïvely believed that simply placing learners in a group would result in collective learning. She expected engaged conversation—high-quality, purposeful student talk; instead, she got awkward silence. Similarly, middle school history teacher Lisa Brooks planned a small-group discussion activity in which her students would explore the essential question "How did post–World War I Europe set the stage for World War II?" She reviewed a collection of curated resources with her students, then released them to formulate a group response and defense. And what happened next? "They just sat there in silence. No one talked. My class, which is very chatty on a daily basis, was simply sitting with a group of their peers looking awkwardly at each other."

Whether they are deployed in 7th grade U.S. history or high school algebra or a 2nd grade classroom, all collaborative learning tasks should be set up to give students opportunities to engage in academic discourse around targeted skills, knowledge, and understandings. These tasks should also provide students an opportunity to learn and practice social and emotional skills. Maybe the teacher's objective is to get learners to make inferences about international conflicts or analyze the use of the horizon line in various pieces of art. Maybe it's to explore the role of symbolism in a text, develop a mathematical model for a specific phenomenon, or design a water filtration system. In all cases, completing the task requires students to participate in critical dialogue around the ideas involved. We want them to engage like a collective of historians, art curators, literary critics, mathematicians, and scientists. We want them to be invigorated, to wrestle with ideas and concepts. We want them to communicate, treat their peers with respect, strive to understand one another's perspectives, develop healthy relationships, persevere through challenge, and develop a sense of self. Too often, though, what we get are surface-level conversations where the most probing question students ask one another is along the lines of "What page did you use to find that answer?"

Of course, no teacher strives to put poorly designed experiences and tasks in front of a group of students, but all of us have done so—and typically we only realize this when an activity that looked great in a lesson plan is a painful failure . . . when the questions and conversation prompts we provide are met with crickets instead of the engaged discourse of an SLC. When creating tasks and activities for collaborative learning in face-to-face and virtual learning environments, it's essential to remember how much language matters.

Attending to Language

Language is how humans think. It's how we socialize with others. We use language to acquire, store, and retrieve information. It is the fuel of the human cognitive operating system (the voice in your head); spoken language (and its signed equivalent) is the representation of that thinking. Take, for example, the concept of area in geometry. Even if learners simply engage in plug-and-chug problem solving, each of them has a cognitive operating system that uses language to work through the problem. They might be working in silence, but they are still engaging in internal self-talk: *That side is the length, and I multiply it by this side, which is the width.*

Getting students to perform their internal language of learning aloud helps teachers gain insight into student thinking, but it's also a powerful way for groups of students to drive their thinking forward. Given that teachers strive to have classrooms filled with thinking, it's reasonable that we would also strive to have classrooms full of talk. But consider the following exchange from Amanda Larson's 3rd grade classroom. As you read, ask yourself how much academic language is being used. How much thinking is happening?

Ms. Larson: I was thinking about the life cycle of an insect. Do you remember the life cycle we studied? Malik?

Malik: Yes.

Ms. Larson: What was the first stage in the life cycle? Jesse?

Jesse: They're born?

Ms. Larson: Yes, things are born, but think about the life cycle of insects. Let's try to be more specific in our thinking. What is the first stage in the insect life cycle? Miriam?

Miriam: Eggs.

Ms. Larson: Yes, insects start as eggs. Then they change and develop. They become larva after eggs, right? And then what? What happens after they're larva? Adrian?

Adrian: They're adults.

Ms. Larson: They do eventually become adults, but there's a step missing. What is the step between larva and adults? What is that stage of life called? Joe?

Joe: Mature larva?

And so it goes. The first problem, of course, is the nature of the teacher's questions, which focus strictly on the recall and reproduction of information. The second issue is structural—the teacher is asking questions of individual students one at a time. The result is an utter imbalance of spoken language. Ms. Larson used 112 words, while her students collectively used 8 words. You may have noticed that the teacher used a lot of academic language, which is great. But the degree to which her students did *not* puts them at a disadvantage linguistically, socially, and academically.

What's also missing is any chance for the students to interact with one another. Studies of teacher talk suggest that as much as 70 to 80 percent of instructional minutes are filled with the voice of the teacher, with the percentage increasing at higher grade levels (Sturm & Nelson, 1997). Student discourse is surprisingly rare, even in content areas and grade levels where we might expect it to be common. True *discussion,* defined as academic exchanges among at least three people for at least 30 seconds, occurs rarely in secondary English classrooms, occupying less than two minutes per period (Wilkinson & Nelson, 2013). In other words, in many classrooms, teachers talk and students listen. We are left to wonder about the potential dearth of discourse in distance learning environments and to what extent online instruction may be even more dominated by teacher talk. In either case, that isn't a recipe for engaged collective learning.

Why Student Talk Matters in Learning

All living things communicate, but only humans do so in verbal and written forms. *Discourse* is an umbrella term for the extended verbal and written messages humans use to reason with one another. Forms of discourse include explanation, elaboration, evaluation, argument, and questioning—all of which are recognizable to us as cognitive structures. It's worth stressing that all forms of discourse are interactive and depend on the presence of more than one person. After all, explanation is purposeless if there is no one in need of the information; evaluation is pointless without someone else who will agree or disagree. Stated simply, a student cannot develop the ability to explain, to elaborate, to argue, or to question without opportunities to practice these cognitive structures with others through academic discourse.

Telling isn't teaching, and students cannot learn by listening alone. They need to try new knowledge on for size if they are to take possession of concepts and apply them to new and novel situations. Academic discourse is the means for this kind of experimentation.

The goal, then, is to provide learning opportunities that transfer the use of academic language from the teacher to students' collaborative learning groups. In practice, this means being deliberate about task design, providing the scaffolding students need to build the skills of discourse, and then gradually releasing the responsibility of student talk to the students themselves. Talking is one way that students come to understand the content, and, thus, opportunities for talking should be included in the instructional design of learning.

In the gradual release of responsibility instructional framework (Fisher & Frey, 2014), opportunities for student discourse abound, and this discourse facilitates learning.

Facilitating Discourse for Learning

For those who aren't familiar with it, gradual release of responsibility is a four-phase process that begins with a teacher establishing the purpose of a lesson and modeling the desired learning. Over time, students assume more responsibility for this learning, moving from being participants in a modeled lesson to apprentices in shared instruction, to collaborators with their peers, and then to independent performers. Figure 2.1 provides a graphic representation of how purposeful student talk factors into each stage of the gradual release of responsibility model. These instructional moves are equally crucial in a face-to-face classroom, in blended learning, or as part of distance learning. In the sections that follow, we note the ways in which talk can be integrated into each stage.

Focused Instruction

The teacher's first task is to establish the purpose of instruction in students' minds as clearly and coherently as possible. Students must grasp why they should engage with the lesson and how they will be expected to use the information they'll encounter to accurately perform the tasks they will be given. Additionally, a coherent statement of purpose helps students access their background knowledge of learned concepts in order to build schema to support the newly introduced concepts. In other words, we go from *the known* to *the new*. Presenting students with clear learning intentions and success criteria signals to them what they will be learning and how they will know they have learned it (Fisher, Frey, & Hattie, 2016). When the purpose is not clear, students may complete a number of tasks and not assume any responsibility for their own learning. In the students' minds, it's "I'm doing this because I was told to, not because it matters to me."

We have found this to be even more important in distance learning. The practice we now recommend is to include learning intentions and success criteria at the beginning of every online lesson. However, these are not useful if they are passively read by students. To engage in active learning, students

FIGURE 2.1

Purposeful Student Talk Within the Gradual Release of Responsibility Instructional Framework

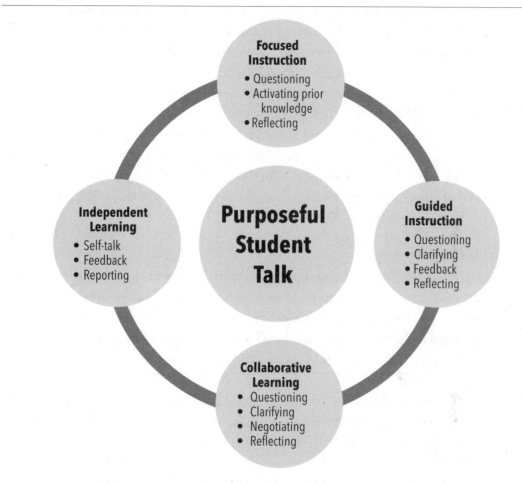

self-assess their knowledge and skills at the beginning and end of the lesson and submit it using the polling feature on the learning management system. Think of these tasks as entrance and exit tickets. They provide the online teacher and all the other students with an understanding of the needs of the group and how their learning is evolving.

During focused instruction, teachers model the behaviors, skills, and strategies they expect to see from their students. This modeling is based on the established purpose and provides students a mental example they can call upon when they are asked to complete tasks in another phase of instruction. Questioning can be a feature of this instructional phase, but its point is primarily to activate students' background knowledge. For example, a 10th grade biology teacher might ask students to talk about cell life with their table partners before explaining cell division to them. During focused instruction, teachers also model the use of academic language by engaging in think-alouds, shared readings, read-alouds, lectures, and other whole-class events. After modeling, students can reflect on what they learned through both writing independently and talking with a partner. Exchanges where teachers model a wide range of strategies and students participate as partners help students to internalize the interactive format along with the new information. Over time, students will develop the ability to perform these tasks independently; these early-phase exchanges provide them with time to practice in supportive situations that encourage them to use language to own and share their thoughts and developing understanding.

Guided Instruction

Although clarifying purpose and modeling tasks help students to start assuming responsibility for their learning, they need guided instruction to be successful. During guided instructional events, teachers elicit student talk as a way to figure out what students know and what they still need to know. This is an opportunity for teachers to use questions, prompts, and cues to help students complete tasks.

The particulars of guided instruction should always be informed by the assessment information teachers glean from these interactions: what do students understand, not understand, or partially understand? Although guided instruction is teacher-led, this does not mean that students are not talking. They use talk to ask questions—of the teacher, of peers, and of themselves. They use language to clarify understanding, provide feedback to a partner, and reflect on their learning. This phase is a priority in a hybrid or distance learning environment, as guided instruction is best accomplished in live learning (face-to-face or synchronous). For schools utilizing a weekly calendar of some face-to-face sessions coupled with remote learning, guided instruction remains a premier pedagogical tool for forwarding learning.

Here is an example. In her discussion with a group of students struggling with the concept of photosynthesis, high school science teacher Maria Grant used a series of questions and prompts to increase understanding.

Ms. Grant: Some of you thought that plants ate soil to grow. This is a very common misconception that we should talk about further. Do you remember the video we saw about photosynthesis? What role did soil play?

Destini: Well, it wasn't about the dirt. It was about the sun and carbon dioxide.

Andrew: And how the plants make oxygen for humans.

Ms. Grant: Plants make oxygen for humans?

Andrew: Yeah. Well, I guess that they'd make oxygen even if there weren't humans.

Michael: It's called a by-product. Plants don't make oxygen for humans. They just make oxygen.

Ms. Grant: And what is left, once they've made this oxygen?

Destini: Carbon. They take in carbon dioxide and then give off oxygen, so carbon is left.

Ms. Grant: And what do you know about carbon?

You can see here how guided instruction provides an opportunity to engage students in thinking without telling them what to think. It's also an opportunity to scaffold students' understanding before asking them to complete tasks independently.

Collaborative Learning

In this phase of instruction, students have opportunities to work together while the teacher monitors their progress and provides needed support. Student talk takes center stage as students work together in face-to-face or virtual structures such as reciprocal teaching, literature circles, and partner discussion. They talk about tasks and ideas, and they question one another. They negotiate meaning, clarify their own understanding, and strive to make their ideas comprehensible to their peers. It is well worth the investment to teach students three to five collaborative learning routines and use them frequently so that they can be easily deployed in distance learning. When students are familiar with the logistics of the routines you regularly use, they can focus less attention on the mechanics and more on the learning.

Critically, collaborative learning conversations incorporate academic language as a necessary means of focusing on and delving deeper into content. This phase is particularly important for English learners, as it provides an opportunity to practice and learn academic language (Frey, Fisher, & Nelson,

2013). As we like to say, "You don't get good at something you don't do." If English learners are not using academic language, they're probably not learning academic language.

Independent Learning

It might seem strange to suggest that talk plays a critical role during independent activities. But think about the self-talk you engage in when you complete a task. Some of this self-talk (inner speaking) occurs in your mind; some is vocalized. Again, thinking occurs as we use language, making this type of talk an important aspect of learning. As students work independently, they may also use talk to acknowledge and discuss input on their work and give feedback to others. Reporting out after independent work may require a more formal register of language than that used during collaborative activities.

Well-structured independent learning tasks should build confidence. By the time students have reached this phase, they should feel prepared for the task, especially when completing it asynchronously, outside the company of the teacher. After all, the purpose is clear, and the teacher has modeled how it is done. There has been time for collaborative work with peers, and any necessary guided instruction has been provided. With the students now at the level of competent novice, the purpose is to help them refine and become more expert. (After all, isn't this how you learned to be a teacher?)

Independent learning becomes the ultimate way to build self-esteem through competence. Self-efficacious learners drive their own motivation to take on new concepts, because they know they have learned in the past and can do so again. Confident learners are more likely to complete independent tasks because they know they can complete them successfully. Too often, students have not had the modeling, guided instruction, and productive group work necessary to be successful independently. But those who have completed this instructional cycle learn from experience that independent learning is fully in their power.

A Checklist for SLC Task Design

Student learning communities (SLCs) are driven by confident collaboration. The experiences and tasks that engage SLCs allow each individual to make meaning (Schlechty, 2011), and this individual meaning-making empowers every learner to engage in collective discourse with the rest of the learning community.

Meaning-making comes from learners doing three things: (1) developing cognitive representations of the content, concept, or idea; (2) finding patterns within the content, concept, or idea; and (3) invoking buy-in or interest (Medina, 2008). The opportunity to exchange dialogue with peers about the main idea of a particular text (developing representations), examine similarities and differences across pieces of text and how main ideas are presented (patterns), and engage in this learning using high-interest text (buy-in or interest) helps students to make meaning of their learning. Each of these components of meaning-making is enhanced when students have opportunities to use academic language.

Deep learning is often impossible without student talk, and high-quality student talk is not likely to happen without well-designed experiences and tasks that promote this kind of meaning-making. Therefore, teachers must ensure the tasks and experiences intended for student learning communities

- Mobilize the skills of individuals as they work collaboratively;
- Have the right level of challenge and capitalize on the value of productive failure;
- Are authentic and motivate learners by allowing them to see the value in the collective learning;
- Promote each team member's feelings of connectedness to the collaborative team; and
- Depend on the team leveraging the skills, expertise, and background knowledge of every individual.

A well-designed experience or task is what sets an SLC in motion. The critical question, of course, is how do you know the task is well-designed for collaboration?

Mobilize the Skills of Individuals for the Collective Benefit

Collaborative experiences and tasks should ensure that students are contributing to the success of the group. Of course, individuals have different skill sets, but the point of a student learning community is to share skills with others and learn from one another in the process. Ivan Dale Steiner (1972) developed a taxonomy of group tasks that provides guidance for teachers as they decide which tasks to use. This model has three categories: component (or divisibility), focus (quantity or quality), and interdependence (combinational strategies).

The **component** category directs teachers to consider whether or not the task has subcomponents that can be identified and then individually assigned. *Divisible tasks* are those that can be parceled out and given to individuals. *Unitary tasks* cannot be further separated and require either the group to work together or one person to complete the task while others watch (or disengage).

The **focus** category asks teachers to consider whether the task's priority is quantity or quality. Is your concern how much the group will produce or how well they will produce it? *Maximizing tasks* focus on greater quantity, whereas *optimizing tasks* focus on greater quality. Imagine a group test. If the stated goal were to get as many questions right within a set amount of time as possible, and partial credit could be earned for partial answers, the group would focus on maximizing the number of responses and getting as much done as possible. However, if points were deducted for incorrect answers, the group would likely focus on optimizing their responses: answering only those questions they were confident in their ability to answer correctly. Of course, there are many group tasks that are *not* tests, but you get the point.

The final category in the group task taxonomy is **interdependence**—the various ways in which individual contributions to a group might be combined. As we will see later in this chapter, interdependence is a hallmark of group learning. Steiner's model lays out five task types that support interdependence:

- **Additive tasks:** Each member contributes individually, and the individual parts are combined for the group task. An example would be a presentation created by a group with the clarification that each member is permitted to go off and create a slide or two independently; they do not need to work together to accomplish the task. The risk with additive tasks is that they often fail to foster the dialogue necessary for student learning communities to flourish. There is a temptation in distance learning to use additive tasks that students can complete on their own and then assemble as a final product. But without opportunities to dialogue, learning across members is limited. Consider adding periodic group check-ins so that students must interact intermittently. This might be accomplished through the chat function of the learning management system, by using a video discussion tool, or through a collaborative online document.

- **Compensatory tasks:** Group members average their individual recommendations and reach agreement about an overall recommendation or solution. An example would be students in an art class who are taught critique techniques, asked to develop scoring criteria, and then provided several pieces of art to evaluate independently. Each student scores the piece using the group's agreed-upon criteria, then the group reassembles, discusses members' individual scores and the rationales behind them, and eventually reaches consensus on a group or average score.
- **Disjunctive tasks:** The group selects one person's answer to represent the thinking of the group. An example would be a group having to come to agreement on the strongest "pro" and "con" statements to kick off a debate about lowering the voting age for national elections. Each member of the group supplies an idea, but only one is chosen for the first round of the debate.
- **Conjunctive tasks:** Group members all contribute to the final product, which sounds really good but can be problematic if the performance of the group is judged by the weakest contribution. Team sports are a familiar example of conjunctive tasks—and the inherent pros and cons. Either the team wins, or it does not. Everyone on the team either wins or loses. An academic example would be something like a competitive task at a Model UN event. Students in each group are incentivized to work hard to prepare their peers, knowing it's a win-or-lose situation.
- **Discretionary tasks:** Members of the group determine what each member's contribution will be and how to combine the individual contributions to produce the best group effort. An example would be a performance from a group of 4th graders that brings to life a section of the history text they are reading. They assign one another roles, but task execution requires them to practice the written script, refine their timing and presentation, and ultimately perform the skit.

Consider this exchange between three students in a face-to-face high school biology class as they attempt to understand the findings of a lab experiment, and how the individuals' contributions drive the task execution—and open it up to interesting new avenues of exploration. Three days earlier, the students had collected saliva samples from their mouths and cultured them in agar dishes. Other dishes contained samples swabbed from other surfaces in the classroom (lab tabletops, the door handle, etc.). The task was conjunctive, as the students had to contribute to the discussion and reach agreements about what to submit in their lab report.

Jake: Man, that's gross [pointing at dish]! Look at all this crud in my mouth!

Kelly: I've got the same thing. There's stuff all over it.

Jake: Bacteria.

Maria: Exactly. Look, you can trace the swab marks.

Kelly: But compare it to the room samples we collected. There's way less bacteria on the room sample collection plates.

Jake: So what does that say about the comparison?

Kelly: Well, our mouths are way more disgusting than our classroom.

Maria: Yeah, but is that really the conclusion? We have to write it up in the lab report.

Jake: OK, yeah, it's more than that. We can say that based on our samples, there was more bacteria present in human mouths than on classroom surfaces.

Kelly: But we can't comment on whether the bacteria from our mouths or the classroom are harmful.

Maria: Right! We don't know that yet.

Jake: Well, that's what I want to know. There might be less bacteria on the classroom surfaces, but what if it's more harmful? How could we find that out?

Kelly: You know what Mr. Walsh will want. We gotta write up a hypothesis.

Jake: Yeah, but it would be cool! Let's find out how we can test these samples for dangerous bacteria.

Plan for Productive Failure

Failure is underrated. Now, before you close this book in disgust, let us explain. We are not suggesting you present students with a task that is so difficult that they immediately give up. We're saying that a task that offers a challenge or a problem to solve makes deep learning possible. It's the wrestling with a task that causes students to rely on one another. A spirit of community can bloom when a group collectively faces a complex challenge. This joint attention to a problem generates solutions for that problem—a clear result. It's also a way to help students build valuable social-emotional skills like persistence, resilience, and determination.

Take a moment to imagine yourself stuck in a massive traffic jam on a freeway. To make matters worse, your lane is ending, and cars are jockeying for position as they squeeze over to complete the merge. Chances are, you are either a "lineupper" or a "sidezoomer" (Gorney, 2008). The lineuppers are patiently waiting their turn; typically, they don't want to let those rude sidezoomers into the lane. The sidezoomers, on the other hand, are utilizing the available space to get ahead, never mind the line. So, who's right? The answer, it turns out, is that the traffic flows most smoothly when the lineuppers and the sidezoomers work cooperatively, with a minimum of braking and speeding up, to ensure that everyone gets in the lane. Think of rice moving smoothly through a funnel. Tom Vanderbilt, author of *Traffic: Why We Drive the Way We Do* (2009), makes this point: ants never get into traffic jams.

What's this got to do with failure and student learning communities? Everything, if you view the issue of merging lanes as a problem, but the *kind* of problem that isn't likely to result in utter defeat. When the traffic's moving along just fine, you really don't notice your fellow drivers. But when the merge lane looms ahead, you start paying closer attention to them. The best result occurs when everyone cooperates to get the job done. This principle has been confirmed by both traffic engineers and queuing theorists (who knew there was such a job?).

Even though most of us have not formally researched queuing theory, we nonetheless understand its principles. You have been stuck in traffic, and you've either been the patient/indignant lineupper or the assertive sidezoomer. At some point, you've probably also witnessed, experienced, or read about the failure of effectively queuing—accidents, horn honking, road rage. The solution, cooperative queuing, makes sense to you precisely because you have faced the problem before. You've learned, after all the trial and error of experience, what the best way really is.

Now, let's talk about how failure plays an important role in learning. To learn collaboratively, students need to be presented with a problem that might result in an incorrect answer, a failed experiment, or an inaccurate conclusion. If success is guaranteed, learning is impossible. Collaborative learning occurs when students recognize they've got a challenge to tackle and are ready to do so. There is an entire research base on the importance of productive failure as an essential element of productive group learning. When the task is structured so that it is complex but not impossible, learners outperform those in groups that have tasks that ensure success (Kapur, 2016).

Ensure Tasks Are Challenging

The possibility of failure does not in and of itself ensure challenge. All of us make mistakes that involve simple tasks (e.g., forgetting to bring a file to a meeting, tripping on a curb, incorrectly calculating a tip on a restaurant bill). Nor is ensuring challenge simply a matter of making a task more difficult to complete. *Difficulty* is a measure of the amount of effort or time required. For example, doing 50 additional math problems beyond the standard assignment might present a high school student with a greater degree of difficulty (more time is required, and it's necessary to sustain focus for longer), but 50 more of the same kind of problem doesn't add complexity to a task. *Complexity* is a measure of the number of cognitive steps needed to complete a task, the amount of prerequisite knowledge required to complete it, and even the possible number of ways it might be solved (Webb, 1997). That same high school student is probably going to find a rich mathematical task that requires the use of statistics and pre-calculus to be complex for all of these reasons.

Generally speaking, an open task is going to be more challenging than a closed task, especially in the sense that it provides the group with opportunities for meaningful discourse. *Closed tasks* yield a single answer and offer little room for discussion, consensus building, or debate. *Open tasks* offer many possible entry points and solutions and allow for different perspectives to emerge. In Chapter 1, we shared a collaborative writing task on traditional Native American food sources; that is one example of an open task. Although the task was bounded, the possible outcomes could vary. Closed tasks might spark compliance and the shared goal of completing the assignment, but they offer little in the way of new learning. You may have witnessed the divide-and-conquer approach student groups adopt when the task offers little in the way of necessary interaction. Open tasks foster student learning communities; closed tasks inspire the divide-and-conquer approach.

Identify Opportunities for Motivation

Task motivation is more than just a willingness to do something. It involves the appraisal or judgment by a learner about whether the task is feasible, useful, and enjoyable (Boekaerts, 2002). Examples of task-related appraisals include the following:

- **Success expectations:** Can I meet the desired outcome?
- **Task utility:** How would I benefit?

- **Task difficulty:** Do I know how to approach this?
- **Task enjoyment:** Will I like doing this?

Group task appraisal continues after a task is completed, as learners gauge their own performance as well as the accomplishments of the group. In the absence of guidelines for how to reflect on their progress, they likely will link their success or failure to luck, rather than examining the role played by effort, the quality of contributions to the task, and individual or group decisions. When that happens, a very important social learning opportunity is lost.

Obviously, insight into students' task motivation can be extremely valuable for teachers looking to refine task design. However, it can be difficult to gauge and often requires some investigation on the part of the teacher to collect feedback from students about their perceptions of the task. We have discovered that the reflective questions about classroom tasks that Glen Poupore (2013) used with college undergraduates work equally well with younger students:

- Did you like the task? Why or why not?
- Was the task difficult or easy? Which parts and why?
- Were you comfortable or anxious while doing the task? Which parts and why?
- Did you like the topic of the task? Why? (p. 102)

Elementary teacher Dylan Hughes started using these questions soon after he shifted to distance learning. "I realized I needed the feedback," he said. "Teaching remotely has been a new experience for me, and I quickly found that some of the nonverbal signals I relied on in the classroom weren't there." After pausing for a moment, he continued, "Now that I think about it, I made lots of assumptions about what my students were learning. These questions get them thinking reflectively, but I'm really the one who benefits. Taking the time to ask for reflections has been giving me real-time feedback about what's working and what isn't."

Reflective questions can be included at the end of a written task to be submitted, as an exit slip for individuals to provide feedback, or as part of a debriefing discussion after a task is completed. There's another bonus to posing questions like these to students: your willingness to seek feedback communicates volumes to your students about their value, their self-governance, their autonomy, and their place in the learning community.

Foster Group Cohesion

Social connectiveness is vital in collective learning tasks performed by SLCs. Teams in general work better when there is a shared motivation to complete the task; such groups typically outperform those who do not share a collective motivation (Kozlowski & Ilgen, 2006).

Shared motivation may be enhanced or diminished by the group's *cohesion*, which is the members' feeling of commitment to one another. As social beings, cohesion and connection to others influence many groups—from family and friendship groups to those in the workplace, in recreational activities, and in school. Consider the times when you have been involved in a game or a project but felt that another person wasn't as invested. Whether playing a board game or cleaning the gutters on the house, the perception that someone else is going through the motions affects the degree of enjoyment you experience . . . and your task performance. Although motivation is cognitive, as one appraises the task, connectedness is affective: it comes from perceptions and emotions.

Social cohesion builds throughout childhood and adolescence as prosocial skills such as helping and sharing develop and children become increasingly better at perceiving the thoughts and feelings of others. Young children need opportunities within tasks to build social bonds. Team roles that promote these skills include the materials manager, the recorder, and the timekeeper. We sometimes add a "spy" role on a team. This person's job is to seek help on behalf of the group, whether from the teacher or from another group. The "spy" role works in a virtual environment, too. While the group is in a virtual breakout group, the "spy" can send a message to the teacher to "drop in" on another group, then take back information. Each of these roles is meant not only to assist the team in working more efficiently but also to foster the affiliation members have for each other.

Although older students may not require formal roles, attention to cohesion remains crucial. A major principle of SLCs is that collective decision making must be present (Roberson & Franchini, 2014). The possibility of failure and the relative challenge of the task contribute to an SLC's level of cohesion, but restricted decision-making opportunities are also important in drawing the SLC together. Ask groups to arrive at consensus, not just complete a task. The process of having to come to consensus promotes their affiliation and social cohesion as they draw together as a team. Roberson and Franchini's (2014) suggestions for different types of group assignments can be used to insert an element of consensus seeking into any task, in any content area. They are listed below, along with examples:

- **Ranking.** Rank the following solutions in order of their plausibility.
- **Sorting.** In the envelope on your table are strips of paper, each listing a statement about X phenomenon. Sort them according to the four theories we have been studying.
- **Scoring.** Read the following excerpt. On a scale of 1 to 4, assign a score that indicates how successfully this writer has applied X principle.
- **Sequencing** (chronological, procedural, logical, or narrative). Place the following events in chronological order. Place the following steps in the order that represents the most effective procedure for solving X problem.
- **True/false.** Evaluate the following statements and decide as a team whether they are true or false. Be prepared to explain and defend your team's answers.
- **What does not belong?** Look at this diagram that lists 10 items. With your team, select the 5 items that have the greatest impact on X phenomenon.

Require Positive Interdependence

David Johnson and Roger Johnson's (1990) seminal work on cooperative learning has influenced a generation of teachers seeking to further the learning and social growth of their students. The principles of cooperative learning are critical if the work is to be productive, and the first principle is clearly understood *positive interdependence*. The task or project must be designed so that the participation of every member is necessary for the completion of work, and no one in the group can get by with doing no work at all. In addition, the job or task should capitalize on the variation among group members to maximize individual strengths. Johnson and Johnson explained that this interdependence comes in several forms:

- **Goal interdependence,** or a "sink or swim" approach that requires that everyone in the group learns
- **Resource interdependence,** distributing materials in such a way that no individual member has everything needed to complete the task
- **Reward interdependence,** ensuring that each member earns an equal share (e.g., a group grade)
- **Role interdependence**, where all members understand their role in partial completion of the task.

Keep in mind that getting everyone involved and contributing is not the same thing as achieving a positive result. We're reminded of *A Million Penguins,* a "wiki-novel" project sponsored by Penguin Publishing and De Montfort University in Leicester, England. Over a five-week period, nearly 1,500 people collaboratively wrote and edited a novel that has been widely described as terrible. (Our favorite sentence from the first paragraph: "Crashing tides sounded groans of discontent.") Researchers on the project noted that this project drew a crowd but never created a community (Mason & Thomas, 2008). Collaboration is necessary, but it's not enough in itself; SLCs should also produce results and achieve learning outcomes.

Task Design in Action

In designing a task template called "Cube It," 4th grade teacher Theresa Czarnopys drew on the principles of challenge, motivation, connection, interdependence, and productive failure. "I believe it's imperative that all students have an opportunity to express not just their thoughts, but also their confusion, misconceptions, and doubts," Ms. Czarnopys said.

Here's how her "Cube It" tasks go. After completing a reading, her students move to their respective SLCs. Someone in each group rolls a six-sided, multicolor die to determine which discussion question they need to answer. Each of the six questions Ms. Czarnopys provides encourages students to describe, analyze, and apply knowledge, as well as to take a stand on the topic, reinvent the reading, and choose a different perspective. Groups typically have time to discuss their ideas for one or two of the questions. The emphasis is on gaining understanding of the text by using and building upon the ideas of peers. In Figure 2.2, you can see Ms. Czarnopys's "Cube It" questions relating to a text about the California Gold Rush.

After the period of in-group discussion, each group shares their question and their thinking with the rest of the class. At the completion of the activity, students rank-order the questions in terms of difficulty, which in turn provides the teacher with feedback she can use in designing future collaborative learning. Over the course of the year, Ms. Czarnopys wants her students to learn the content, of course, but she also wants them to develop social and emotional skills while they learn about themselves and each other. SLCs help her pursue both goals.

FIGURE 2.2

A Task Designed to Promote Collaborative Learning

Cube It!

⚀	**Describe it**	In one year's time, San Francisco grew from a city of 900 people to a whopping 56,000 people! Describe how this happened so quickly, giving as many details as possible.
⚁	**Analyze it**	What were some of the problems that resulted from such a huge growth in the number of people in California during the Gold Rush?
⚂	**Apply it**	Many people came to California as a way to get rich quick, with no intention of mining gold. What were some of the different ways that people made lots of money as a result of the Gold Rush?
⚃	**Take a stand**	Do you think it is better to get rich quickly or to stick to a slower, but safer method of making money? Why?
⚄	**Reinvent it**	If you had lived during the Gold Rush period, what other ways might you have been able to make money without having to mine the gold?
⚅	**Choose a different perspective**	Do you think you would have wanted to move across the country to California to search for gold? Or, as a member of a family, would you have argued against it? Why?

A practice such as Cube It can be easily adapted to a live virtual session, with each group weighing in on their decisions. Importantly, the outcome is that students have regular experiences with listening to one another in small groups as well as the in whole class. In addition, they gain further experience with interacting with one another, an important skill we've all come to appreciate in our own virtual work meetings!

Task Transformation

If you have taught for more than a few years, chances are good that there are some tasks you return to again and again. We hope that this chapter is inspiring you to give those tasks a facelift.

The Department for Education and Child Development in South Australia is in the midst of a 10-year initiative to create a world-class education for all of its students. Part of the initiative is to help teachers "transform" tasks they have been using in order to better build knowledge, meet high expectations, and help students develop the social skills they need to be successful. Teachers across the state are being trained to examine their tasks systematically to find ways to elevate the complexity, challenge, and quality of peer interactions by considering four conditions:

- **From closed to open.** How might the existing task be strengthened through creating multiple entry points and pathways, as well as multiple perspectives and solutions?
- **From information to understanding.** How might the existing task be improved by asking students to explore different ways of knowing by applying critical thinking skills (e.g., compare and contrast, generalize, make connections, and identify relationships)?
- **From telling to asking.** How might the task be more motivating by asking students to explore before explaining, leveraging student voice, using Socratic questioning, and fostering dialogue in the classroom community?
- **From procedure to problem solving.** How might the task foster interdependence and social cohesion by allowing students to identify the problem to solve, providing them insufficient information at first, giving them only some of the steps, or including some irrelevant information?

The chart in Figure 2.3 provides an overview of the task analysis and design process. The goal set for teachers in South Australia is to design tasks so that students are doing more thinking while deepening knowledge about themselves. It's a good goal for us all. Stretching students intellectually and metacognitively also grows their capacity to take wise and positive action.

Moving Forward ...

SLCs are a way to leverage the collective wisdom of the group to ensure deep learning. To function, they require well-designed experiences and tasks that engage learners in academic discourse, provide the right amount of challenge and the necessary motivation, and allow students to connect with and relate to other members of the team. These tasks also need to be engaging for every team member.

FIGURE 2.3

Transforming Tasks

Strategies	Techniques			
From closed to open	Different perspectives	Many entry points	Many pathways	Many solutions
	Have students explore different points of view in the task.	Have students work backwards by beginning with the outcome.	Ask for one problem to be solved in multiple ways.	Ask questions that have many solutions. Add or remove constraints.
From information to understanding	Many ways of knowing	Compare and contrast	Make connections, find relationships	Generalize
	Ask students to show what/ how they know in more than one way.	Ask students to identify similarities and differences.	Have students make meaning by asking them to connect pieces of information.	Ask students to construct general rules by identifying patterns.
From tell to ask	Socratic questioning	Explore before explain	Use dialogue	Student voice
	Ask questions that help students dig deeper.	Ask students to try their ideas first.	Ask students to interact and build meaning through learning conversations.	Ask students to decide how they might do this best.
From procedure to problem solving	Students identify the problem to solve	Provide insufficient information at first	Don't give all of the steps	Include some irrelevant information
	Present a provocation and ask students to determine the problem to solve.	Give a perplexing problem and slowly provide information as needed.	Provide multistep problems and do not state all the steps.	Give additional information that is not required to do the task.

Source: Adapted from *"Transforming Tasks: Designing Tasks Where Students Do the Thinking,"* by Government of South Australia, Office of Education, Department for Education and Child Development, 2019. Copyright 2019 Government of South Australia, Department of Education.

It's a tall order, but it's absolutely within every teacher's power. Transforming the collaborative tasks you assign to support a student learning community begins with reflecting on past collaborative learning experiences and tasks and how students responded to them.

The following questions are a good place to start, and you can use them going forward to monitor interactions in your classroom and inform your task design decisions.

1. Did your collaborative teams find meaning in their learning and bring their individual meaning to the understanding or completion of the task? How do you know?

2. Did each individual member, and thus the collective group, remain engaged in the learning, even when experiencing a challenge? How do you know?

3. When encountering a challenge, did your groups maintain their shared agreement of success without compromising or lowering those criteria for success? How do you know?

4. Were all members of every group able to leverage their skills, expertise, and background knowledge toward the understanding or completion of the task? How do you know?

Supportive Relational Conditions That Empower Learning

When 16th century English poet John Heywood wrote "many hands make light work," he wasn't thinking about student learning communities (SLCs). But he undoubtedly had some significant outcome in mind—something important to do that was more easily done together.

So did teacher Gabriel Larouche, when he designed a task for learners to collectively explore the representation of classic literature in modern films. He explained, "I know all of my students are familiar with *The Lion King*. I want them to see that *Hamlet* follows a very similar literary theme, with characters and topics. Can they find other commonalities?" Prior to the day's lesson, Mr. Larouche spent time intentionally creating the groups for his collaborative learning activity. "I want to make sure that I put together complementary groups—where every member brings a particular strength to the group that makes them an essential part of the team."

Mr. Larouche has recognized a key feature of collaborative learning, considered by many to be its defining quality: *positive interdependence* (Johnson & Johnson, 2009). For SLCs to thrive, members must recognize that their individual success is inextricably linked to the success of every other member of the group. In other words, students in an SLC grasp that every member's contribution is necessary, and the success of one depends on the success of all. This is what Ann Friedman and Aminatou Sow (co-hosts of the podcast *Call Your Girlfriend*) call *shine theory*—"I don't shine if you don't shine." Commitment to collaboration with others requires that every individual make a unique contribution to create the conditions for success. In SLCs, students are both dependent on and obligated to their peers. When students need one another to succeed, joint tasks become mutually beneficial situations in which students are helping themselves while helping their peers.

However, it is important to remember that "outcomes" are not just about task completion. Students who mistakenly think that the only thing the teacher cares about—the only thing that matters—is whether the job is done are missing out on the learning opportunities inherent in the SLC process. Teachers who foster a false dichotomy of complete versus incomplete tasks overlook the nuances of what happens inside the mind of learners as they work in tandem with others. These teachers also miss valuable opportunities to develop social and emotional skills in students. In contrast, teachers like Mr. Larouche intentionally design tasks to be more than a list of steps that learners rush through to completion. Mr. Larouche explained:

> I want my learners to relate to each other in their groups so that they engage in the process of literary analysis and are better able to comprehend foundational works of literature. Some of them struggle with the process part of collaboration, but it's an important social skill that will serve them well.

Students who possess strong content knowledge but lack the social skills to participate positively in the process of group work can struggle in this learning environment. Think of all the academically capable students you have had who reliably respond to the announcement of collaborative work with an immediate "Can I work alone?" One who stands out in Doug and Nancy's memory was Tarik—knowledgeable and academically skilled but always wanting to work on his own, never with others. It took a while to realize that Tarik was wary of the social relationships expected in group learning; he was anxious about the *process* dimension of these tasks.

We will return to Tarik later, but now we want to proceed to the main point of this chapter, which is that designing a great task and then putting students into groups is not enough. Educators must also consider how we can create the supportive relational conditions that are crucial for successful student learning communities. Here are the essential actions involved:

- Modeling the relational conditions we want to see in learners;

- Using *knowledge emotions*—surprise, interest, confusion, and awe—to build students' social skills and peer support;
- Teaching social sensitivity and social cohesion; and
- Creating a physical environment that enhances student interaction.

It may seem daunting or difficult to spend time on building the supportive relational conditions necessary for deep collective learning, especially when there is a sense of urgency to improve achievement and prepare students for the rigors of higher education and the demands of the world beyond the classroom. The apparent paradox of devoting time and attention to the social climate of the face-to-face or virtual classroom is easily justified: it fosters an atmosphere of cooperation, collaboration, and enthusiasm for learning. Building a sense of community results in greater productivity, not less, and it leads to higher goal attainment, not lower. Intuitively, we know that cooperation, community, and positive peer relationships support long-term success, and research bears this out:

> From infancy to old age, having friends and relating successfully to other people is associated with desirable outcomes in virtually all human domains: school, work, parenthood, adaptation during life transitions, coping with negative events, and maintaining self-worth and emotional well-being. (Roseth, Johnson, & Johnson, 2008, p. 237)

The coronavirus pandemic of 2020 has given most of us an even deeper appreciation of this truth. The quality of our professional and personal relationships has taken on a new importance. The skills needed to promote and maintain relationships are learned through family interactions and school interactions. In this chapter, we'll be looking more closely at the ways in which teachers can foster the supportive conditions that promote positive connection and collaboration in SLCs.

Modeling Desired Ways of Relating and Interacting

Teachers model, whether it's intentional or not. In order to create the conditions for SLCs to thrive, teachers must model the dispositions that allow groups to work together effectively and productively. For example, if we want our students to become proficient at giving suggestions and providing explanations within their SLC (we do), we need to show them what those behaviors look like in context.

Webb, Nemer, and Ing (2006) studied the connection between the types of interactions used by teachers in middle school mathematics classrooms and those that occurred among students when subsequently working in small groups. They discovered that although the teachers emphasized group norms (e.g., no putdowns, listen to others) and provided class-building activities to foster collaboration, their students rarely offered specific help to one another—because this was an action seldom exhibited by their teachers. Instead, the "help" these students offered typically came in the form of telling a peer the answer without providing an explanation of how to arrive at it. In other words, students mimicked what their teachers had modeled, not what the teachers had intended students to do. Webb and colleagues noted that "changing student behavior in the classroom without a concomitant focus on changing teachers' accustomed style and content of instruction" resulted in students who "seemed to use the skills they perfected in a didactic learning environment in the collaborative environment without much modification" (p. 108).

The danger of such group interactions is that they do not foster the kind of learning skills that SLCs need to function. Collaborative learning is designed to give students the opportunity to consolidate and refine their learning and, through that work, build everyone's understanding. This is not going to happen when a group member struggling with a concept is simply told the answer. Answer-giving also reinforces the kind of negative experiences that inhibit learning, especially the negative self-talk that occurs when a learner feels "too stupid to get it." Last but not least, this type of interaction fosters the notion that filling in the answer, or completing the task, is what's most important. As educators, we know that deep learning comes from processing information and searching for answers. But learners who doubt their learning capacity, known as *agency* in the social and emotional learning area, are not going to be successful, even in the presence of other learners. There is a biological function that gets in the way.

The Biology of Learning

Many of the mechanisms that can either inhibit or encourage learning are built into the human cognitive architecture. One particular part of this cognitive architecture, the amygdalae, is a pair of almond-shaped neuronal clusters located deep in the temporal lobes of the human brain. Studies of the amygdalae in neuroscience are ongoing and rapidly evolving, but current thinking suggests that one of their primary functions is to process learning formed through emotional events (especially fear, reward, and uncertainty) and to further consolidate these memories as they move from working (short in duration) to long-term (more permanent) memory (see, for example, Tyng, Amin, Saad, & Malik, 2017). This makes sense; survival itself may depend on remembering what triggers fear, what brings reward, and what may or may not be a threat.

Think of the amygdalae as the security desk of a busy office building (the brain). People flow in and out of the building all day long and travel to various floors depending on the nature of their business. However, this security desk, like most security desks, is equipped with both security guards (the neurons in the amygdalae) and a screening system that vigilantly checks for any sign of threat (i.e., fear and uncertainty). When a danger is perceived, the security personnel deny access, temporarily stopping the flow of other incoming traffic until the perceived threat is addressed. The security desk and screening system collect data to enable recognition of similar threats in the future, essentially creating a "wanted poster" to remind themselves not to be fooled again. Similarly, the security system prioritizes the "big shots" who might be approaching the entry. Let's say the building owner's name is Mr. Reward. Whenever Mr. Reward is spotted walking up the sidewalk, the security desk makes sure that he is able to enter the building quickly and is whisked up the elevator to his destination. Mr. Reward's pathway is cleared so that nothing will delay his travel to any place in the building.

The Classroom Implications

Now let's bring this back to classroom learning and student learning communities. As educators, we don't speak about fear and reward pathways—we talk about *affective filters*. According to the affective filter hypothesis, certain emotions, especially negative ones like fear and embarrassment, interfere with a learner's ability to acquire and process academic information (Krashen, 1987). Like the physiological flight–fight–freeze response to threat, a student who experiences negative emotions during a learning event will either escape or freeze up. Learning still takes place, but it's directed at neutralizing the threat itself—that is, students learn new ways to check out of or avoid the work. This could be acting like they don't care (because it leads to fewer expectations or a diminished role in the group) or being disruptive (because it sometimes gets them kicked out of the group entirely). On the other hand, events associated with positive emotions contribute to a heightened state of academic learning. Imagine the student who feels safe to take a risk, shares her thinking aloud, and then receives supportive comments from peers about her thinking, both in terms of their agreement as well as their follow-up questions. Unlike the student who is learning how to avoid challenging learning situations, this student is learning to welcome them.

The effects of negative and positive learning events are related to the positive interdependence that SLCs need to thrive. On the one hand, joint collaboration occurs when there is a shared set of goals, which lowers the level of fear ("I'm not in this alone") and increases the anticipation of accomplishment ("I can see we're making progress"). The reward doesn't have to be external; when someone is invested in achieving a goal, progress toward it can be a reward in itself. Whether viewed biologically, by examining the role of the amygdalae, or psychologically, as an affective filter, the results are similar: threats interfere with academic learning because attention and memory shift to the negative stimuli. Therefore, to create the conditions that support a student learning community, whatever students find threatening needs to be removed or reduced and replaced by something they find rewarding.

Siham Sayed, who teaches 7th grade mathematics, knows that some of her students find the pre-algebra content intimidating. "I can see the fear in the eyes of some of them on the first day of class," she said. "They're coming into my math class already believing that they can't do it. And fear is not going to help them learn." Ms. Sayed also knows that SLCs are essential to her students' success. "In my class, *math* is a public discussion of mathematical thinking," she explained. "If students can't talk with one another about their reasoning, there's no hope that they'll gain the knowledge they need." Ms. Sayed is also concerned about the unique social needs of young adolescents, who are quite attuned to the perceptions of their peers. "Being 12 years old is hard under the best of circumstances," she acknowledged. "Being afraid of math is just one more way they engage in negative self-talk."

With these factors in mind, Ms. Sayed habitually models and reinforces how mathematicians help one another figure out complex problems. Two or three times a week, she presents students with a solution culled from a homework assignment. Her selection criterion is straightforward: an incorrect solution with some really good mathematical thinking embedded in it. She tells them this is her "favorite mistake" and works through an anonymous student's solution, thinking aloud about the correct elements of the solution, as well as where the student might have gone wrong:

The big push is this: I want them to see the logic behind the incorrect answer. I'm not selecting answers that have a calculation error, because those are easy to solve. I want them to appreciate all the good math that went into it.

Ms. Sayed also intentionally works to build students' capacity to mediate each other's thinking in their SLCs:

I ask them what questions they would have for the anonymous student. Not the *answer*, but questions. It's so important that they know how to be open to the ideas of others, especially when they're wrong ideas. I want them to know how to ask those questions instead of just giving the person the right answer because that feels less awkward to them. The emotional part of learning math? That starts with me.

Not all emotions contribute to learning. In fact, quite a few—such as anger, fear, and boredom—have a negative influence. Students who experience or witness these negative emotions with peers are not likely to learn. Their security system is going to deny access. If we want effective SLCs, we must cultivate the kind of emotional response that enables students to learn at optimal levels.

Using Knowledge Emotions to Build Learning Pathways

Emotions are transitory. Humans can experience a variety of emotions even within the time span of a few minutes, and many of the emotions we feel result from our appraisal of a situation (Lazarus, 1991). Although we make these judgments independently, they can be influenced or even overruled by our peers. For example, a student who greets a challenging task with positivity and confidence might help a nervous peer who had judged the task "too hard" to reevaluate the situation and feel differently. In this way, when working in their learning communities, students can mediate the emotional reactions of their peers. What seems confusing to one student might be the source of excitement for another. To make the social-emotional learning connection more transparent, students need to recognize and name their emotions and learn to regulate those emotions. Doing so in the presence of peers is one of the benefits of student learning communities.

The four *knowledge emotions*—surprise, interest, confusion, and awe (Silvia, 2020)—work like glue to help information or insight stick. Like all emotions, they are automatic responses to personal appraisals of a situation at hand. The circumstances students find themselves in can stop some learners in their tracks and encourage others to move forward. As teachers, we must be mindful of the emotional component of students' collaborations and develop opportunities for students to interact with their peers as they work through the range of emotions they experience.

Surprise

When something unexpected occurs, we are more likely to recall it long after the event is over. The internal appraisal that generates surprise is something like *I did not see that coming! This is new and different!* Science teachers familiar with how surprise can ignite learning often introduce steps to build surprise into lab experiments. For example, asking young children to experiment with lenses to determine how they work can spark a rich discussion within an SLC. The same can happen when students are reading. A group of students who are working together to read *Bud, Not Buddy* (Curtis, 1999) may be surprised to learn what happens when the main character sets out to find his dad. Consider the value of having some students predict what will happen and discuss their ideas with peers. Then, when the story's surprise is revealed, the groups will *want* to talk about it, forming memories of the content, its significance, the author's craft, and the power of collaboration.

Interest

Whereas surprise follows from appraising a situation and finding it novel, interest is kicked off by appraising both a situation's novelty and determining that it is something we can cope with. *This new thing—I'm ready to think about it and explore it!* In other words, interest in something reflects how prepared we judge ourselves to be to meet the challenge we perceive it to present (Silvia, 2020). Understandably, interest plays a very powerful role in collaborative environments and is one of the main determiners of whether or not a student will engage or stay on the sidelines.

Consider that a student who is just learning English may very well be surprised by what happens during his group's magnet experiment. However, if he lacks the receptive and expressive academic language to participate in the exchange of ideas, his perceived ability to cope with the task's requirement will probably be low, and so will his interest in engaging with the task. The group's disposition to make sure he is included and understands can make the difference in the learning experience for everyone involved.

Confusion

Confusion is the emotion that results from four appraisals of a situation: *Is this new and unexpected? Can I cope with the challenge it presents? Do I understand what's going on? Are others as confused as I am?*

The notion of *productive failure* is predicated on confusion (Kapur, 2016). When a group struggles with a task, the best recourse is for everyone in the group to retrace their steps and think through the problem again using a different tactic. The failure is *productive* because it ultimately leads to understanding. Of course, if there is too much confusion and it spills over into frustration and anger, the group is going to give up altogether. But when confusion is present at optimal levels, there is the potential for the group to think more creatively (Silvia, 2010). A group that encounters a confusing poem, for example, might give up too readily if the team doesn't have the supportive relationships necessary to rally their collective spirits. A teacher's supportive statements can help in these circumstances, too. A high school English teacher who announces, "This was a confusing poem for students last period, but they figured it out by working together" alerts students to the fact that confusion can be expected and is surmountable. Another way to ensure groups react constructively to confusion is to equip them with the skills they need to seek help.

Awe

Awe comes from two very different appraisals. The first is that something is vast, and the second is that it is uncommon—far outside usual experience (Silvia, 2020). The best approximation of it might be *Wow . . . this is blowing my mind. I never thought of this before.* Awe is perhaps most familiar as a profound aesthetic response to music or art, an incredible landscape, or a spiritual event, and it is most often experienced alone (Shiota, Keltner, & Mossman, 2007).

Naturally rarer than the other knowledge emotions, awe can also be more difficult to conjure in a classroom setting. However, awe can be used as a spark for an SLC, especially in group reflection. For example, the awe that may result from a virtual field trip to a planetarium to see the vastness of the night sky, or from a musical or theatrical performance, should not be squandered. This is an opportunity for students to come together to debrief their impressions and experience the communal nature of a shared awe-inspiring situation. The knowledge they gain from this interaction can expand students' understanding not only of any connected content but also of themselves and one another.

Here's the takeaway: Learning is not simply a series of cognitive actions to be accomplished in a completely logical and reasoned way. Emotions play an important role in learning, and as social beings, students are attuned to their own emotions and those of others in their collaborative learning group. The social sensitivity to the emotions experienced by all members of the SLC contributes to the social cohesion the group uses to accomplish tasks and learn from and with one another.

Social Sensitivity and Social Cohesion

Social sensitivity is the ability to sense and understand the feelings of others. *Social cohesion* is the glue that binds a group together and is a product, in part, of the social sensitivity of the members of a group. Social sensitivity typically develops with age, and older children as a group are more socially sensitive to others than are younger children. Teachers can support the development of social sensitivity by discussing characters' feelings when reading books and by pointing out the facial expressions of actors in multimedia presentations. They can also intentionally notice and address social sensitivity in the classroom. This can be more of a challenge in a distance learning setting. When meeting with students on a virtual platform, give voice to what you are noticing. For example, "Adam, you got a puzzled look on your face when I was explaining binomials. And so did several other people in this session—it was not just you! That is telling me I need to find out more about the questions many of you have so I can do a better job with this topic." Intentional acknowledgment of the emotional climate in a virtual classroom signals to students that they are not alone in their experiences, even though they may be separated physically.

Of course, face-to-face classrooms do not guarantee the social sensitivity and cohesion of the group. Many of Julianna Hargrove's 4th grade students know each other from previous years in the elementary school where she teaches. Although the school enjoys a low mobility rate among its student body, Ms. Hargrove understands that familiarity is not the same as knowing someone. In fact, a concern she has had is that students' familiarity with their classmates may have dulled their social sensitivity. "I've overheard students say things like, 'Oh, Aiden always gets mad about stuff like this,' in a dismissive kind of way," Ms. Hargrove told us. "I want to reset their understanding about one another." So, in her efforts to help her 4th graders sense and understand the feelings of others, she introduced a personal interview as part of a larger social studies project students will be conducting on local history. Here's a look into her classroom.

On the board, Ms. Hargrove has written the purpose of the lesson:

- *Learn about your classmates.*
- *Ask questions to find out information.*
- *Make a brief oral presentation describing your partner.*

As she tells the students what they are going to learn, she also tells them *why*—that in this classroom, they work together as student learning communities. "To work effectively as a team," Ms. Hargrove reminds them, "you need to know about each person as an individual, even if you've known them since kindergarten." She adds:

> Asking unexpected questions can get you surprising answers from people you thought you already knew. This interview is your opportunity to learn new things about one another, make connections, and get ready for future interviews with people out in our community.

Ms. Hargrove begins by explaining that good interviewers ask questions that encourage the other person to say more than yes or no, and to speak in more than one-word answers. She refers to a chart where she has written, *What do you like to do when you are not at school?* She reads the question aloud and answers it for herself, saying: "Baseball." She explains that, as an interviewer, she would want to learn more about this answer and might ask questions about what position the person plays, what team or players they like, and so forth. "I could follow up with this question," she continues, writing *Who do you talk to about baseball?*

Ms. Hargrove stresses to her students that interviews are more than the words a person says:

> It's also about how they say it and the facial expressions they use when they say it. So, when I'm making notes, I also want to write down how I think the person is feeling. Are they happy or

excited, or does it seem like they are thinking about a memory that is making them a little sad?

To model the interviewing process, she asks Trent to come to the front of the class and help her demonstrate. Each student has a handout with interview questions and room to take notes (see Figure 3.1). Ms. Hargrove asks students to look at the first question and listen as she interviews their classmate, Trent. One by one, she asks the questions and Trent responds. Throughout, Ms. Hargrove reminds the students to notice how she looks directly at her interview subject, nods her head to show interest in his answers, asks additional questions that are not on the handout but follow from Trent's replies, and makes notes to help her plan what she will say later to formally introduce her subject to the class. "I'm making notes about what he says," she explains, "but I am also adding information about how he is saying it." Ms. Hargrove provides an example: "When I asked Trent how he got his name, his face lit up and he got really happy when he told me that story about how it was the name of the taxicab driver that took his parents to the hospital the night he was born!"

With the modeling complete, Ms. Hargrove forms pairs of students for the activity. She asks students to line up in order of their birthday months ("January babies here! OK, now February babies next . . ."), and when the line reaches all the way across the classroom, she directs students to double back, so that a second line forms running parallel to the first. Eventually, each student is facing another in the parallel lines (Kagan, 1994). Ms. Hargrove uses this configuration as a way to partner students randomly for the interview because she wants her students to know *all* their classmates better, not just those in their immediate social network.

While the students interview each other, Ms. Hargrove reminds them to make notes about the emotions their subject exhibits. Later, when the interview partners introduce each other to the class, she asks questions about the information they are sharing and what they noticed about the feelings of the person they interviewed. Molly, who interviewed Serena, says this:

> When I was talking to Serena, she got kind of . . . what's that word we learned last week about when you're missing someone? Oh yeah, *wistful*. She was wistful when she talked about her

FIGURE 3.1

Guided Personal Interview Task

| Interviewer: _____ |
| Interviewee: _____ |

Question	What did they say?	How did they say it? What feelings did you notice?
What is the story of how you got your name?		
How long have you lived here? Where is a place you would like to live someday?		
How many brothers and sisters do you have? What would you ask someone who has lots of siblings or who is an only child?		
What do you like to do when you are not at school? Who do you talk to about it?		
What is one of your favorite books? What kind of person would you recommend it to?		
What's your best subject in school? What advice would you give to someone who wants to get better at this subject?		
What is a career (job) you would like to learn more about? Why?		

grandma and how she liked it when they lived near her. But they moved, and now they are far away.

"How did you know Serena was feeling that way?" Ms. Hargrove asks. After checking her notes, Molly explains:

Serena's voice got a little quieter, and she was looking up more instead of looking at me. So that made me think she was thinking about a nice memory, but one that she wished could happen again, like when India Opal was thinking about her mom [a reference to *Because of Winn-Dixie,* a book the class had recently read].

Ms. Hargrove pauses to let Molly's observations linger, then says, "We sure can learn a lot about each other by paying attention to people's feelings as well as their words."

———————————

The opportunity for students to learn more about one another can increase their social sensitivity. And when students connect with the both content and the experiences of their peers, they also strengthen their social sensitivity. When groups have strong social sensitivity, they are much more likely to be productive and learn more. In fact, one of the hallmarks of student learning communities is members' ability to understand the feelings of others.

Providing Intentional Support for Peer Relationships

The social cohesion of members of an SLC is also crucial to its success. In their meta-analysis of 148 studies involving 17,000 middle school students, Roseth and colleagues (2008) found a strong positive association between peer relationships and academic achievement. These peer relationships are cultivated through cooperative—rather than competitive or individualistic—goals. The authors' findings are a reminder that an exclusive focus on academics without equal attention to social learning diminishes the former.

The good news is that if you are being intentional about providing emotional support to your students, they are benefiting. By *emotional support,* we don't mean counseling. We are referring to the warmth and responsiveness you exhibit in your interactions with students. And thanks to tens of thousands of classroom observation analyses from preschool to high school, we can identify four dimensions of teacher emotional support: genuinely caring about students, respecting them, understanding their feelings, and being someone they can depend on (Pianta & Hamre, 2009).

Adolescents are especially sensitive to the ways their teachers convey caring. Sincerity matters, and so does the care you show others in the class. It isn't solely about the way you communicate caring to an individual student; they are watching closely to see how you treat their classmates, including those who struggle. Students are particularly good at figuring out which students teachers don't like, and the consequences of this perceptiveness can be destructive. If they believe a teacher's negativity toward certain students is unwarranted, they will deem it unfair and be less likely to trust or learn from that teacher. If they agree that teacher's negative treatment of certain students is deserved, they will accept it and follow suit. In these cases, students who aren't favored by the teacher can become outcasts, and this ostracization will undermine efforts to create an emotionally secure learning environment.

Displaying emotional support for all students provides the class with the foundational means to work with each other in ways that promote learning. It is an old adage that the teacher sets the temperature for the class—and five decades of research back up this practical knowledge. Students will rally around a previously marginalized student when the teacher signals that child's value. This is especially true when students recognize that every person has unique positive qualities and flaws—and *both* can be accepted.

For teachers, fostering positive peer relationships means making an investment every day in the following practices:

- **Maintaining a positive climate,** which includes a shared positive affect, enthusiasm, positive comments, and encouraging students to listen to one another;
- **Displaying sensitivity to students' needs,** which includes recognizing their difficulties and emotions, resolving questions and problems, and providing help and guidance; and
- **Showing a positive regard for students' perspectives** by encouraging student ideas and opinions, connecting content to students' lives, encouraging movement within the classroom, and incorporating peer sharing and group work (Pianta, Hamre, Hayes, Mintz, & LaParo, 2011).

These are all actions that teachers can take immediately to develop the conditions for supportive relational conditions among students. That's more good news: You don't need to cross your fingers and hope the kids this year like one another well enough to work together. Whether your students will become an effective SLC doesn't depend on their character—it depends on you. You are the one to jump-start the action and build the skills to sustain it.

Keep in mind that these same three practices are just as important, perhaps even more so, in a distance learning environment. Consider how difficult it can be to engage some students virtually. The barriers and inequities that get in the way include problems with access to Wi-Fi and digital devices, but we certainly don't need to contribute to the problem by operating a virtual learning space that is emotionally chilly to students. Students' reluctance to participate or even check in because they don't find the experience to be emotionally or psychologically rewarding gives new meaning to the phrase "remote learning."

Remember Tarik, the student who always asked to work alone? Doug and Nancy figured out pretty quickly that this academically accomplished teen struggled with peer relationships, and this limited his learning. Tarik had a history of strained peer relationships from the previous grade. His peers knew he was academically talented but found him to be overbearing in group interactions. They recognized that they needed to raise his status in the eyes of his classmates. So they actively sought opportunities to positively comment on Tarik's attempts to engage in speculative thinking. When he issued pronouncements of absolutes that tended to end conversations, Doug and Nancy followed up with questions that encouraged him to continue discussion with others in the class. Reponses from them like "Interesting! Why do you think that is the case?" invited Tarik to think beyond what he already knew. "What do you need to ask to better understand?" was another go-to; it always led him to deeper reflection. As the other students witnessed these new ways to engage with Tarik, they were able to see what was lying below his surface bravado. They also got to see that his teachers valued Tarik's insights and were willing to dig a bit deeper expose his thinking to others.

Doug and Nancy also did some reengineering of the classroom environment to help all the students in the class develop collaborative learning skills.

Engineering the Classroom Environment

The classroom environment, whether physical or virtual, plays an important role in supporting the development of SLCs. We'll consider both, starting with the physical. Does the physical environment in your classroom support positive interdependence? There are two very practical things you can do to help ensure it does.

Promote interaction through flexible seating

Primary and elementary teachers often have a rug area in the room to bring students together for whole-class reading or discussion where students can easily talk with partners. In addition, these classrooms often have students seated at small tables to form groups of four. This is an arrangement we find in many elementary classrooms—children sitting in groupings of four or six around two or three tables that form a pod. Many high school classrooms, on the other hand, seat their large numbers of larger students in rows of desk chairs, or in larger table groups. And middle schools tend to be just that, in the middle. Some classrooms use tables and some use desk chairs. These configurations become more complicated when physical distancing requirements are needed. Let's look at how flexible seating can improve interaction in two types of scenarios.

When physical distancing isn't required. Success of an SLC depends on thriving social sensitivity. How can you configure your classroom so that students can see each other as they collaborate? We recommend seating students in groups of four around tables that are small enough to facilitate conversation, yet large enough to accommodate group projects and supplies. There are a number of ways in which this physical arrangement supports effective teaching practice. First, placing students in groups of four lends itself to a variety of configurations. Students can work with a partner, and then two pairs can easily form a group of four. Students can pair with the person seated next to them or across from them. Purposeful seating like this allows you to partner students in different ways (e.g., heterogeneously or homogeneously) for different reasons without having to ask them to physically move. Four also seems to be a good number to promote engagement for all students—enough voices to express different ideas and perspectives, but not so many as to be intimidating to students who are not yet completely comfortable sharing or speaking up.

Flexible seating applies not only to configurations but also to the relative number of students in a group. Not every group has to be the same size. Instead, adjust the size of the group to meet the needs of its members. This is exactly what Doug and Nancy did for Tarik. Their classroom had a range of table sizes, from four to six members. Initially, they made sure that Tarik's group was smaller than others, because social arrangements were difficult for him. Think of a juggler keeping all the balls in the air, and you get the idea: Tarik benefited from having fewer relationships to juggle. Over time, they "grew" his group to continue to stretch his ability to maintain social cohesion with a larger number of people.

Obviously, seating arrangements are constricted by practical reality. Teachers must work with the furniture they have in their actual classrooms. Many schools are in the process of replacing desk chairs with tables and chairs, but funds are limited and change takes time. Teachers who are intent on promoting SLCs, however, can find ways to accomplish this.

For example, consider Don Riley's biology classroom, where most of the real estate is occupied with rows of permanent lab stations jutting out from the sides of the room. Because Mr. Riley has no choice but to seat students in rows, four students to a row, he has to be creative in his planning. Sometimes he has students in one row turn their chairs to face the students behind them, forming two groups of four with the lab station between them serving as a table. Sometimes Mr. Riley asks his students move about the room, talking with a partner about the observation charts on the walls. Still other times, he has students move their chairs to the area in the front of the room for a "fishbowl" demonstration. For this activity, students choose to stand on one side of the room or the other based on their stance on a controversial topic, or they go to one of the four corners of the room based on their choice of a topic or task.

When physical distancing is required. Teachers have to rethink classroom arrangements when public health directives allow for full-time or intermittent face-to-face instruction under distancing guidelines. Physical distancing of student learning communities is impractical, as the vocal volume needed to talk with partners means that other groups would be disturbed. Instead, use online collaborative tools in the physical classroom when students are meeting as SLCs. They can host their discussions using learning management system (LMS) features that allow you to assign them to their own chat rooms, contribute to collaborative online documents, and respond to one another using video tools. These are ideal opportunities to teach students how to collaborate virtually, as the teacher is present to coach and troubleshoot as needed. And students can carry knowledge of the logistics of operating new tools into their remote learning.

These tools can be a springboard for launching the SLC's efforts. Rashida Armstrong introduced her high school anatomy and physiology students to huddle boards (see Figure 3.2). "[Huddle boards] come from the medical field and are used to figure out what needs to be done for the day, especially as nursing shifts change," she said. In hospitals, these are physical whiteboards that outline the priorities on the floor. "I introduced them last year for the first time," Ms. Armstrong said.

At the beginning of extended projects that will take more than one day to complete, the teacher introduces the task in person and then has the groups meet virtually. Ms. Armstrong explained:

> They use the whiteboard feature on the LMS. There are three sections: *Not Started, In Progress,* and *Done.* They track their progress on their project to make sure they are addressing all the aspects they need. Across the bottom of their huddle board is a category called *Roadblocks* so they can track problems and address them. They meet up at their virtual huddle board at the beginning of the lesson to figure out where they are and make decisions about what needs to happen next.

FIGURE 3.2

Project Collaboration on a Virtual Huddle Board

	Not Started	In Progress	Done
Tasks	Handout Ethical issue video We have to finalize what our ethical issue is going to be Giving blood if you are gay? Access to health care, especially Black and Latinx population	Video on circulatory system ~~Info gathered~~? ~~Storyboard made~~? Filming? Need 2 PSAs American Heart Assn web campaign? Treating blood pressure? Still looking for another one	PSA #1 Risks of vaping on heart (Tobacco Free CA)
Roadblocks	We can't make the handout until filming is done	Having trouble finding something–we want it to be for teens Ask Ms. Armstrong for advice?	

In one of Ms. Armstrong's units, she assigns SLCs specific body systems to study, asking them to produce several collaborative products, including an informational video with a handout to share with classmates, a second video where members of the group discuss an ethical issue related to their assigned system, and three associated public service announcements. "The huddle boards have been valuable for groups that are doing some things together and other things separately," she said. "It seems to help them to talk through tasks and problems instead of just assuming someone else in the group will figure it out."

Promote interaction through visual support

The physical and virtual arrangement of the classroom can facilitate communication; visual supports provide a further valuable scaffold. Some classrooms have virtually nothing on the walls other than the fire escape plan and the bell schedule. Some are filled with so many charts, pictures, rules, and samples of student work that items are dangling from the ceiling; the thought of adding more visuals seems impossible. The same is also true in distance learning. The visual organization of the LMS should alert students about what is to come and what is expected of them. However, it should not be so cluttered that it is difficult for students (and their families) to navigate. When it comes to communication, supports for interactions should be apparent. If you want your students to enact the social skills needed in an SLC, it is helpful to remind them of the language they should use.

Although the work of the classroom is necessarily academic in nature, it can be difficult for students to explain their thinking and learning to others. Members of an SLC need to be able to compare and contrast ideas, ask questions, and describe phenomena. It's useful to provide students with sentence starters related to the different types of thinking necessary in any learning environment. We recommend posting "language of learning" posters (see Figure 3.3) around the room or on your LMS page for live sessions, referring to these, and modeling use of the phrases. Also consider providing table tents displaying language frames to support students during their collaborative learning or making these available by posting them in their virtual breakout rooms as they meet in small groups.

These accountable talk frames contribute to the governance of the norms of academic discourse needed in an SLC, and they require students to furnish and ask for evidence to support their statements. This ensures rigor and moves the conversation from task-oriented to concept-oriented learning. In a classroom filled with accountable talk, students ask one another about their thinking and build on the responses of others. They cite evidence, ask for elaborations and clarifications, and extend understandings by using the statements they have heard from their classmates to form new ideas.

FIGURE 3.3

Language of Learning Poster

Language goal	What is it?	What does it sound like?
To instruct	Giving directions	"The first step is . . ." "Next, . . ." "The last part is . . ."
To inquire	Asking questions	Who? What? When? Where? Why? How? "What do you think?"
To test	Deciding if something makes sense	"I still have a question about . . ." "What I learned is . . . ."
To describe	Telling about something	There are descriptive words and details.
To compare and contrast	Showing how two things are alike and different	"Here is something they both have in common . . ." "These are different from each other because . . ."
To explain	Giving examples	"This is an example of . . ." "This is important because . . ."
To analyze	Discussing the parts of a bigger idea	"The parts of this include . . ." "We can make a diagram of this."
To hypothesize	Making a prediction based on what is known	"I can predict that . . ." "I believe that ___ will happen because . . ." "What might happen if . . . ?"
To deduce	Drawing a conclusion or arriving at an answer	"The answer is ___ because . . ."
To evaluate	Judging something	"I agree with this because . . ." "I disagree because . . ." "I recommend that . . ." "A better solution would be . . ." "The factors that are most important are . . ."

Source: From *Content-Area Conversations* (p. 96), by D. Fisher, N. Frey, and C. Rothenberg, 2008, Alexandria, VA: ASCD. Copyright 2008 by ASCD.

Students take quickly to this kind of language when it is part of the climate of the classroom. The guidelines also help to prevent conversations from going astray. Consider this collaborative learning conversation in May Hirano's 2nd grade class as four students discussed an ant diagram during a science lesson. She asked her students to discuss the ways an insect communicates and to decide what body parts an ant uses to communicate.

Kristina: Well, I know they touch.

Roberto: But how do you know? And you can't just say you know because you know! [*Requesting evidence*]

Kristina: OK, I know 'cause I seen them wave their . . . their . . . what are those pointers on their heads?

Ting: Right here [points to diagram]. Antennae. [*Offering evidence*]

Kristina: Yeah, antennae. They use their antennae to touch each other.

Alejandra: Oh yeah, we're supposed to use that word. Ms. Hirano wrote it on the board—*antennae*. They touch their antennae to see each other. [*Using ideas from others*]

Ting: Do they have eyes on their antennae? Can you show me? [*Requesting evidence*]

Alejandra: [Examining diagram closely] I don't see eyes here. [*Giving evidence*]

Roberto: The eyes is here [points to label that reads *eyes*].

Kristina: Oh yeah, that's right! They can see! They use their eyes to see. [*Using ideas from others*]

Ting: Look how teeny their eyes are. They must not see a lot of stuff.

This is a typical accountable talk interaction among young children. They still think and speak like the 7-year-olds they are, but the difference is that they are listening to one another instead of speaking in parallel. Notice too that the conversation hasn't wandered from the topic; Ms. Hirano's students are accustomed to working together like this. And keep in mind that exchanges like this can occur in face-to-face classrooms or in live virtual sessions. The task goals and accountable talk guide the academic discourse of the group without imposing an artificial structure that limits students' thinking.

Moving Forward . . .

Classrooms where students thrive are classrooms where students know each other and feel safe, supported, and part of a community. Creating a climate of collaboration is one component of effective pedagogy for developing SLCs. It is also a way to ensure that we are creating equitable classrooms.

Classrooms are filled with students from all around the world, from different cultures, language backgrounds, and socioeconomic levels. The world of work for which students are ultimately being prepared is equally diverse. Learning to work with others is necessary for success in school and in life. This has become even more apparent with the shift to working from home in a virtual environment for so many professionals. Meetings still happen, planning sessions still occur, and teams debrief their progress in virtual spaces rather than in offices. In order for students to gain the social skills to work with others in an academic environment, teachers must foster the supportive relational conditions needed to practice those skills within an inclusive climate—one based on the belief that everyone has something of value to contribute.

The following questions are a good place to start, and you can use them going forward to monitor interactions in your classroom and inform your decisions relative to the relational conditions necessary for student learning communities to thrive.

1. Have you modeled the supportive relational conditions that you expect your students to exhibit with their peers?

2. Do you notice your students experiencing emotional reactions to their learning? Do you ever prompt them to name those emotions and regulate them? In your classroom, do peers support one another in regulating emotions?

3. Do your students exhibit social sensitivity? How do you know? Are the student learning community groups cohesive? What actions might you take to increase their social cohesion?

4. How does the physical or virtual learning environment in your classroom support the relational conditions necessary for student learning communities to thrive?

Shared Agreements
About Success

A shared understanding of the purpose for learning, both individually and as a learning community, is vital for students to move forward in that learning.

Think for a moment about the last time you didn't know the purpose of something you were asked to do. Perhaps you were asked to go to the store and get some things. What store? What things? Without knowing that, how would you be able to have a successful shopping trip? Not knowing what success looks like is a sure route to frustration and, more than likely, to failure as well.

Now let's say that you were asked to go to the grocery store to get supplies for making a birthday cake. Much better! You can comply with this simple task, but what would help you really engage with it? What if you were asked which grocery store in your area stocks the highest-quality dairy and eggs? What if you were asked what your favorite cake recipe was? What if you were asked for decoration ideas, or even asked to help decorate the cake so it would look spectacular? What would move you from simple compliance with the task to full engagement in the activity such that you cared about the execution of each step and were invested in the outcome? Often, it's having a shared definition of success that encourages that shift.

A look inside Cristina Edwards's 5th grade classroom shows us that shift in progress.

Ms. Edwards' 5th graders have settled in for their morning meeting, a routine that kicks off each day and helps to prepare them for the work at hand. After greetings are exchanged, Ms. Edwards turns her students' attention to the day's agenda. First, she reviews the schedule ("You'll be in your art rotation today with Ms. Leong at 1:35"). Next, she shifts to the posted learning intentions, outlining the content, language, and social skills students will explore that day (see the sample in Figure 4.1).

FIGURE 4.1

Individual Content Learning Intentions and Success Criteria

Subject	Today's learning intentions	Today's success criteria
Reading	I am learning about the relationship between main ideas and key details.	• I can identify the main idea in an article. • I can identify key details in an article. • I can explain the relationship between the main idea and the key details.
Writing	I am learning to provide and receive feedback about an opinion essay.	• I can give useful advice about the opinion and reasons provided by the author. • I can identify areas for feedback. • I can use feedback from others to improve my writing.
Math	I am learning to graph fractions on a line plot.	• I can solve problems that involve fractions. • I can justify my approach using mathematics language.
Science	I am learning about the energy flow of desert carnivores.	• I can create a visual representation of energy flow using accurate diagram techniques. • I can use my visual representation to explain relationships in the desert ecosystem.
Social Studies	I am learning about the economic issues that led to the American Revolution.	• I can compare and contrast England's and the Colonies' positions on the issue of taxation.

"Our first question today, and every day, is *Where are we going?*" Ms. Edwards begins. "A map's no good if you don't know what the destination is." She reads the learning intentions aloud and then goes deeper, explaining the success criteria for each of the content objectives. "Knowing where we're headed is how we plan our learning journey," she reminds the class. For the next few minutes, the students ask questions about the learning intentions and success criteria. Then Ms. Edwards guides them to the next step.

> The next big question we tackle every day is *Where am I now?* Given the learning intentions and success criteria today, where are *you* right now? Please take a few minutes to rate yourself in terms of your present knowledge. This will help me with structuring your learning supports today.

To respond to her questions, the class uses a four-point self-assessment system:

1 = This is not familiar to me, and I will need help to understand it.
2 = I'm familiar with this, but I need more practice.
3 = I've got this. I can do it on my own.
4 = I own this! I can help others.

The students enter their self-assessment scores into a digital spreadsheet that Ms. Edwards has set up. It allows her to quickly and flexibly group her students to create heterogeneous groups throughout the day. She makes note of which students might need additional teacher-directed instruction in small groups, beyond the whole-class teaching she has planned. Students also talk with a partner about the results, which are displayed at the aggregate level and not with individual students' names. For example, they note that the lowest average score is for the math success criteria. Armando says, "It's just new for us. We can do it. We have each other's backs." Natasha adds, "We've done hard things before, and I trust you all. This is Room 26. Nothing gets in our way."

Ms. Edwards then announces, "Some of the learning you'll do today is with others. I've also set up some group success criteria for your student learning communities to consider." She reveals the third element of her daily learning map (see Figure 4.2).

FIGURE 4.2

Individual Content Learning Intentions and Success Criteria *Plus* SLC Success Criteria

Subject	Individual learning intentions	Individual success criteria	SLC success criteria
Reading	I am learning about the relationship between main ideas and key details.	• I can identify the main idea in an article. • I can identify key details in an article. • I can explain the relationship between the main idea and the key details.	• We can analyze an article and reach consensus. • We can redirect peers when they are off topic.
Writing	I am learning to provide and receive feedback about an opinion essay.	• I can give useful advice about the opinion and reasons provided by the author. • I can identify areas for feedback. • I can use feedback from others to improve my writing.	• We can ask and answer clarifying questions. • We can provide honest feedback that is specific and constructive.
Math	I am learning to graph fractions on a line plot.	• I can solve problems that involve fractions. • I can justify my approach using mathematics language.	• We can persevere and provide encouragement for each other when the problems are complex.
Science	I am learning about the energy flow of desert carnivores.	• I can create a visual representation of energy flow using accurate diagram techniques. • I can use my visual representation to explain relationships in the desert ecosystem.	• We can take turns and actively listen to each other.
Social Studies	I am learning about the economic issues that led to the American Revolution.	• I can compare and contrast England's and the Colonies' positions on the issue of taxation.	• We can help others who are having difficulty. • We can monitor our body language to show that we are interested.

As the day proceeds, Ms. Edwards returns to the other key questions designed to drive her students' collective learning. For example, after providing initial whole-class instruction in the reading lesson, she says, "I've given you some initial information and practice on linking the main idea and key details in an informational article. Next, you'll be meeting in SLCs to apply this in the science article you have been given. Before we do so, take another look at your individual and group success criteria. What do you plan to do to move your learning forward?" A student named Gibson writes this in response:

Read carefully. Probably read it twice. Circle main ideas. Make a list in the margin so I know the key ideas. Watch out for interesting facts that aren't key details. Check with my team to see if they agree.

By regularly posing questions about moving learning forward, Ms. Edwards helps her students build the metacognitive habit of considering possible strategies to use *before* they tackle a task or challenge. Another thing she does is regularly focus her students' attention on their own learning and how their peers might provide support. It helps to foster students' metacognitive awareness of their current level of performance and their next steps in planning. This is a critical aspect of social and emotional learning known as *cognitive regulation*. A student named Kaia writes this:

I'm not sure I picked the right article. I don't know a lot about energy transfer. So I need to re-read it. But I think I should talk with Mariacarla after I read it b/c she has the same article as me. We can compare our annotations. If we talk together, I might get a better understanding.

Forty minutes later, as the lesson draws to a close, Ms. Edwards invites her students to consider what they have learned. She redirects their attention to the learning intentions and success criteria and asks them to reassess their current status using the same four-point system they used at the beginning of the day. "What did we learn today?" she prompts. "Remember to think about both the content *and* the processes your teams used." Jessica, turning to her group, says, "I learned that I need to listen better. We all have good ideas and I understand this better because of all of you."

Ms. Edwards also reminds the class that before entering their second self-assessment score, they should "check in with your left shoulder partner, using the success criteria for the lesson. Where are you now on your learning journey?" Quinn and Tanner turn to each other. Tanner begins by indicating the success criteria that requires summarizing main ideas and using key details to support them. "I'm not sure I can turn this into a paragraph yet," he says, "but I did identify what I think the main ideas should be, so that's good." Looking at Tanner's annotated article, Quinn notes that although they had read different articles, "I think I'm ready to do that on mine. I could read yours and tell you if it makes sense. We don't have the same one, so I could give you good feedback." A few minutes later, Quinn enters his self-assessment score, a 4; he believes he can help Tanner, who has rated himself a 2, because he feels he needs some more practice.

Ms. Edwards later explained that she and her 5th grade students have invested a lot of time in building the right environment and habits to support collaborative learning, including the mindset that success is something that can be pursued actively and together. After the lesson, she said this:

> At the beginning of the year, we had to spend a lot of time focused on reaching agreements about success. It wasn't familiar to them. But with lots of daily practice, it only takes a few minutes. I hope it's building some habits of mind about how they should be taking control of their learning, not just passively waiting for knowledge to get poured into their brains.

The students in Ms. Edwards's class have come to believe that they will master the learning intentions she presents. They also believe that working together in their SLCs will help them achieve those goals. The takeaway? Meeting the success criteria for the individual and for the group is key to students' collective learning.

The Case for Success Criteria

There's strong evidence supporting the use of teaching strategies that emphasize success criteria. Hattie's (2019a) mega-meta-analysis of success criteria reports an effect size of 0.54, suggesting an influence of more than twice the average influence on student achievement. The strategies in question are "often brief, co-constructed with students, aim to remind students of those aspects on which they need to focus, and can relate to the surface (content, ideas) and deep (relations, transfer) learnings from the lesson(s)" (Hattie, 2019b, p. 18).

The usefulness of success criteria is really twofold. For the teacher, the success criteria are the product-and-process features that signal student progress toward the learning intentions. Thinking back to the design of experiences and tasks that engage teams in collective learning, success criteria should align to the following:

- The specific type or nature of the discourse expected during the day's learning (e.g., explain, give advice, justify, compare, and contrast);
- The degree of challenge reflected by the task (e.g., identifying and explaining, solving and justifying);
- Authentic learning experiences offered during the learning block that motivate learners (e.g., creating visual representations, offering and supporting a personal opinion or perspective, working together to help fellow learners);
- The nature of the interactions and connectedness expected during collaborative learning (e.g., redirect, monitor, encourage, actively listen); and
- The degree of collaboration that is expected (e.g., consensus, feedback on a rough draft).

In addition to signaling progress toward the learning intention, the success criteria are the conduit for making the day's expectations clear to every learner. They provide specific answers to the *Where are we going?* question and highlight the possible difficulties students may encounter (Clarke, 2014). Clear statements in the form of success criteria also provide opportunities for learners to recognize their own expertise, skills, and background knowledge that they can leverage toward their individual success, as well as the success of their student learning community.

Success criteria are truly invaluable in a distance learning environment. Students navigating instructional modules that combine synchronous and asynchronous learning experiences are in danger of getting lost in the weeds without clear and cohesive success criteria. One approach you might take is to post task success criteria in the chat function each time you meet with students in a live function or on the virtual whiteboard in your LMS. As Ms.

Edwards did in her face-to-face classroom, have students complete a self-assessment at the beginning of the session using the polling feature so that you can gain a sense of where you need to spend more time (or less time) to increase the precision of your teaching. Keep these success criteria posted prominently at the top of asynchronous experiences so that students are reminded of their learning. Even better, record yourself stating these to personalize the message.

Back in Ms. Edwards's classroom, with the success criteria in front of her, Kaia recognized that her partner Mariacarla was very good at explaining her thinking; she made a note that this skill was a growth area for herself. Of course, Kaia's ability to pick up on Mariacarla's explanatory strength suggests that Kaia likely possesses strong active listening, which she is leveraging to benefit from this collective learning experience. The student-facing side of success criteria really is crucial. Students who can identify strengths and anticipate challenges they and their peers will face can plan more efficiently to access strategies that will help them succeed.

In the end, of course, it is up to teachers to help students anticipate challenges, identify strengths, and locate the strategies they need to carry their learning forward. With a clear and agreed-upon definition of success, learners can engage actively, efficiently, and effectively in each day's learning. Teachers can support these efforts by giving students opportunities to

- Set goals and reflect on them,
- Link their individual goals to group goals,
- Monitor their own progress,
- Reach shared agreements, and
- Establish and uphold norms with their student learning community.

Let's look at these practices one at a time.

Goal Setting

Ms. Edwards emphasized to her 5th grade students that it's tough to travel anywhere when you have no particular destination in mind. Goal setting, for people of any age, increases the likelihood that a desired outcome will be achieved. Knowing at the start of the journey that you want to arrive in Pasadena, for instance, is crucial unless you enjoy aimlessly meandering through the epic traffic of Southern California.

Academic achievement goals are associated with academic self-efficacy, which should not come as a surprise, given that competence is the foundation of each (Huang, 2016). Students who regularly set goals, gauge their progress, and respond dynamically to changing conditions build a stronger sense of agency over their learning. Students who see learning with peers as essential to their own learning, and who view themselves as contributors to those efforts, will profit from collaborative arrangements. Just as well-designed experiences and tasks promote connectedness and collaboration, shared agreements on success provide the clear, attainable, and measurable goals that help guide collective learning. Examining success criteria and self-assessing their current skill levels relative to those criteria paved the way for Ms. Edwards's students to set personal goals like "Work on being able to explain my thinking more clearly."

Student goal setting should be a regular practice in classrooms. Goals students set for themselves can drive learning in ways that teachers might otherwise only dream about! Think for a moment about a goal you might set for yourself. You set that goal because you see value in achieving it, and you see the value in each step you take along the way, including the kind of less-than-thrilling practice that attaining a worthwhile goal almost always requires. The same is true for students setting their own goals to support work toward collective objectives.

As you will recall, Kaia had a goal of improving her skills in sharing thinking with others. As she said, "I need to slow down a little to figure out what I think so that I can explain it to other people." Kaia also recognized that she was a good listener. She added, "I also have a goal to help my group listen to each other better. Sometimes people say the same thing somebody else just said. Or they take us off topic. If we all listened better, our group would be better."

Success criteria lend themselves to being converted into mastery goals. Unlike performance goals, which are externally oriented (e.g., "I want to get an *A* on this argumentative essay"), mastery goals guided by success criteria are *useful;* they lay out what mastery—the desired outcome—looks like (e.g., "A strong argumentative essay has a clear claim, supporting evidence, and logical reasoning"). The difference is subtle, but important. Mastery goals that are supported by success criteria are empowering. They sharpen students' sense of what they need to do and help them focus on the actions they can take (organize the essay so that there is cohesion among the claim, evidence, and reasoning) rather than what the teacher or other evaluator may or may not do (give them an *A*). Mastery goals also provide learners with ways to monitor their progress and stay on track (e.g., "Am I supporting this claim with related evidence? Does my reasoning make sense?").

However, we can't stop here. Simply setting individual goals related to the main idea of a particular text, fractions, energy flow, taxation in the colonies, or any other topic does not necessarily lead to the collective learning that is the focus of this book. Instead, teachers have to explicitly incorporate a second opportunity for learners to link those individual goals to group goals. This is where the shared agreements on success really elevate the collaborative learning in face-to-face and virtual classrooms.

Linking Individual Goals to Group Goals

Too often, students do not associate their individual learning goals with those of the group. Instead, group activities are just that—something the teacher makes them do without benefit to their own learning. No wonder children and adolescents often have a narrow group goal: task completion. *Get it done, perhaps get it done well, but little else.* Their own learning isn't seen as an outcome, and the potential for learning is lost. To build student learning communities, the success criteria are not limited to the learning that individual students do. Yes, students need to know what success looks like in terms of their individual learning, but they also need to know what success looks like for the group.

For example, here is one of the success criteria a teacher shared during a unit on the water cycle: "I can use the terms *evaporation, condensation, precipitation,* and *runoff* in my explanation of the water cycle." There is nothing wrong with this content-focused success criterion, and we would hope that students would be able to accomplish this as a result of their learning experiences. However, as stated, it does not help students know if they are making a successful contribution to a group's overall effort. Success criteria can also inform students about the ways in which their groups should interact. These success criteria can be "evergreen," meaning that they last for a long time, or they can be task specific. For example, the students in Albert Hueso's middle school online science class know that there are individual success criteria for working in a group. At different times, students may be working on any of the following (see NGSS Lead States, 2013):

- I ask questions to determine relationships between independent and dependent variables.
- I value and respect my fellow classmates, their perspectives, and their learning.

- I construct explanations based on evidence from sources.
- I construct, use, and present oral and written arguments supported by scientific evidence and reasoning.
- I gather, read, and communicate information from multiple sources.

Note that these statements address science practices *and* the skills that support collective learning within an SLC. Mr. Hueso's success criteria communicate the importance of learning in the company of others as a key to success in his virtual classroom.

But groups need goals as well: success criteria that clarify what they are expected to accomplish together. SLC success criteria, like the examples in Figure 4.2 (see p. 59), illuminate both how group members should interact *and* the product they will create to make their collective learning visible. For example:

- We can analyze an article and reach consensus (*group learning* success criteria).
- We can redirect peers when they are off topic (*group interaction* success criteria).

Melinda Katz's 2nd grade classroom provided a clear example of one way to present group success criteria. When we visited, her students were engaged in a social studies unit on food production that covered the roles played by farmers, processors, and distributors; weather; and land and water resources.

The students began the day's group activity having already completed some independent reading and prepared graphic organizers. Ms. Katz explained that their task that day had several parts. First, they needed to use their notes and graphic organizers as reference while creating a poster explaining the process for getting an assigned food item (e.g., milk, bread, eggs) from source to market. Next, they would need to explain their poster to the other groups, respond to their peers' questions, and write questions of their own to ask during the other groups' presentations. Finally, each student would need to write a paragraph about food production. Ms. Katz posted and reviewed the success criteria. In terms of content for individual students, it was "I can explain food production and the different factors that contribute to the food we eat." The group success criteria were "We can share ideas about food production and create a visual representation that shows our collective understanding."

When students accept, take ownership of, or make meaning of the group learning success criteria, they are much more likely to leverage their individual skills, expertise, and background to accomplish that goal—ultimately meeting the success criteria for the benefit of the collaborative team. Having success criteria that only focus on the content learning can undermine students' sense of *collective efficacy*—the belief that working with other people helps them learn more. When students accept the challenge of taking ownership of their learning, they are also more interested in monitoring their progress toward success.

Progress Monitoring

We also have to explicitly incorporate a third opportunity for our learners: monitoring their progress toward individual and group success. Progress monitoring is not just an effective practice for teachers; it is also of great benefit for students. Too often, if you ask students why they earned a certain score or grade on an assessment, their answer is "I don't know." They are not lying. Many students aren't able to identify their strengths and opportunities in their learning to even recognize and adjust their next steps in the learning. Teaching students how to monitor their progress can remedy that and further support their ability to take ownership of their progress and the progress of their peers.

In order for students to be able to monitor their own progress, they need to understand clearly what they are expected to learn. This comes directly from the learning intentions and success criteria. Take the previously shared success criterion associated with learning about the water cycle: "I can use the terms *evaporation, condensation, precipitation,* and *runoff* in my explanation of the water cycle." Individually, learners will invigorate their learning when they have the skills to monitor their own success at using these terms. For example, did they use the terms by simply repeating the definition in a sentence, or are they able to apply the terms in subsequent discussion of the water cycle (e.g., the role of the water cycle in erosion and weathering)? Success criteria related to content, interactions, and products provide all learners with an understanding of where they need to be and then help them to determine where they are, relative to these expectations, as both individual learners and members of a learning community. There are a number of ways that teachers can support students and student learning communities in monitoring their own progress. Two strategies we like are to teach students to (1) chart their performance data and (2) use success criteria to self-assess.

Charting Performance Data

Giving students a visual representation of their performance is a good strategy for engaging them in progress monitoring. When you also give them a rubric with established performance levels, it's even more powerful.

Consider the example provided by Sonja Williams, who teaches an online high school senior-level course called Writing for College. Although the topics of her students' papers change, many of the learning intentions and success criteria remain the same. After students write their first essay, she has them identify two areas on the writing rubric where they have an opportunity for growth. After each paper is returned, Ms. Williams's students review their proficiency levels on the rubric against their targeted areas for growth and chart their progress on the template she provided to them at the start of the semester. She is careful to not have them identify too much to monitor, to ensure that they focus on key areas for growth and make purposeful decisions in their learning to improve those areas. Each student's individual progress template is posted in the assessment portion of the learning management system so it's readily available for reference.

In our conversation with Ms. Williams, she stressed this point:

> Some of my learners may have significant gaps in terms of their achievement, but monitoring progress helps identify incremental growth, thus improving their academic self-esteem. They see that they are making progress and are more likely to make adjustments to the learning when they see that it is paying off.

Ms. Williams also engages her students in a reflection that invites them to think about what they did or did not do to affect their performance level, as well as to identify their next learning step. She explained, "Once my students master a targeted area that they were monitoring, they restart the process and identify a new area to monitor. I think that this helps them see that learning is a process." Using this strategy to have students track their own progress has been associated with significant gains in student achievement (Marzano, 2010/2011).

Critically, the progress monitoring Ms. Williams's students do informs their group processes. Once students have determined the areas for improvement, they meet virtually in goal-alike groups that are fluid and needs-driven.

For example, students who identify that they need more work on developing a clear thesis statement meet together to work toward this goal. Another set of students might form an SLC focused on citing evidence. The groups conduct peer critiques on the identified problem of practice and provide feedback to each other (see Chapter 5). When a group encounters a roadblock, members can consult with Ms. Williams for further guidance. "It's not unlike what they'll encounter in college," she explained. "Study groups saved me, and I want them to gain an appreciation for how their learning can be positively affected by others."

Ms. Williams and her learners succeed not because these students are seniors or even because they are college-bound seniors. Nor can the effectiveness of their collaboration be attributed to having a clear rubric, although that helps. No, the driver for the collective learning they do together is the shared agreement of success, based on clear goals that are monitored intentionally.

Using Success Criteria to Self-Assess

As noted, a learning intention provides students with an awareness of where they are going in their learning; success criteria guide students to achieve mastery of those outcomes.

Juan Diaz, a 5th grade teacher, created a template that allows his students to do just that. At the beginning of each learning experience, he has them write the learning intention in a space at the top of the template. Along the left side of the template, there is a place for them to capture the success criteria. Then, at the learning experience's conclusion, he asks his students to self-assess their progress against each success criterion, using a rating scale he developed. Mr. Diaz also asks his students to provide evidence for why they gave themselves the rating they did, and he asks them to identify the next learning step that would move them forward. He noted that this tool has been invaluable in student-led conferences with their families, as it has bolstered each child's ownership of learning:

> I'm currently hosting these meetings virtually, with the family and their student participating from home. Families are eager to support their child in learning but don't always know how. I love hearing kids talk about their learning directly with their parent. It makes it clearer to families what their child is doing and what the child's goals are.

Self-rankings use a similar approach with success criteria for a unit of study. Jill Hardaway always shares the major success criteria at the launch of a unit of instruction in her 7th grade social studies class. For example, on the first day of a two-week unit on the feudal system in Japan, she identified five major success criteria (see Figure 4.3).

FIGURE 4.3

Success Criteria Self-Assessment for Medieval Japan Unit

Level of challenge (1 = Easy, 5 = Hard)	Success criteria
	I can identify influences of samurai culture on medieval Japan's government and culture.
	I can explain how the clash between Shinto and Buddhist religions sparked feudalism in medieval Japan.
	I can analyze how the roles of military and cultural revolution across Korea and China influenced Japanese culture of the time.
	I can analyze cultural artifacts from medieval Japan and place them in their historical contexts.
	I can trace the growth of trade and urbanization of the time across Japan, China, and Korea.

Ms. Hardaway's students previewed the success criteria for the unit and ranked each on a scale of 1 to 5, from easiest to most difficult. She reviewed these self-rankings to get an idea of where areas of challenge might be for each student. These rankings are also a tool for grouping (and regrouping) for the unit's collaborative tasks. Ms. Hardaway explained:

> As we move through the lessons, I have the students identify where they ranked themselves for each of the success criteria. That way they can readily see what each member believes he or she has to offer to the group. Teams work best when they understand their internal strengths. It's also a way for them to remember that no one is strong or weak across the board. Everyone is a valued member.

The ability to use success criteria for self-assessment is a powerful skill that students can transfer beyond an individual experience, task, or classroom. It's something students can use across their academic studies, in hobbies and leisure activities, at home, and in the workforce. Most employment settings have some process that requires employees to set goals and then monitor their progress. This practice—alongside supportive relational conditions, the leveraging of peer support, and student-led collaboration—builds a skillset that will facilitate successful collaboration well beyond the elementary, middle, or high school years.

We need to note, when describing how to support students in monitoring their progress, that it does take time, and the skill of progress monitoring requires deliberate practice. Unless students have engaged in progress monitoring during some of their prior learning experiences, they will need support and time to become used to applying progress monitoring to the work in your classroom. If students aren't masters of gauging their learning from the onset, don't give up. Rather, focus on ensuring that progress monitoring is an integral part of your classroom culture so that it eventually becomes part of how your students "do business" in your classroom.

Providing Time to Reach Shared Agreements

Simply putting learning intentions and success criteria on the board and reading them to students before the start of a day, a unit, or a lesson will not generate the kind of shared agreements on success that SLCs rely on any more than standing in an empty garage and hoping for a new Cadillac will make one appear. Students need time to focus on learning intentions, think about what they mean, ask clarifying questions, and brainstorm reactions. It's not just a matter of giving students two minutes to focus on each lesson's learning intentions, either; it's about teaching them to take collective ownership of learning intentions as a matter of course, and about them mastering the process for doing that.

Here's a look at how 3rd grade teacher Lorena Gilbert reinforces her students' ability to reach shared agreements. Whenever she introduces a learning intention, she highlights the purpose behind it and draws connections between the intention and her students' needs. Her favorite tool for this is the phrase "I've noticed that . . . ." For example:

> I've noticed that in your writing, there are some words that trip you up. Those words have double letters in them, like *bubble* and *happen* and *channel*. So our learning intention for the spelling lesson coming up is to get familiar with a new spelling pattern: the double consonant followed by a short vowel.

Next, she leaves space for the students to come to a shared agreement:

Would you please take a minute now to talk with your discussion partner about the purpose of this lesson and why we're learning about double consonants? Partners, listen carefully and fix up each other's thinking if you need to.

As her students talk, Ms. Gilbert listens in so that she can get a sense of their understanding. If she hears confusion or partial understandings, she knows she needs to clarify.

At the conclusion of the task, the students have another opportunity to compare their SLC results to the success criteria. Ms. Gilbert revisits the learning intentions to review major points and asks students to self-evaluate their success. As she explained, "I usually have them give me a fist-to-five gesture in front of their chests. A fist means 'I'm lost' and five fingers means 'I completely understand this.' If they're somewhere in between, they show me three fingers."

This familiar formative assessment technique generates feedback about student understanding and identifies which SLCs need follow-up support. If she sees a lot of fists ("I'm lost"), she asks the class to pose questions about what they still need to know. She lists their questions and often uses these for the following lesson's "I've noticed" rationale. "Shared agreements aren't only for the students," Ms. Gilbert explained. "I need to understand where they are in their learning."

Using Norms as Overarching Success Criteria

Academic discourse in any content area during collaborative learning challenges the social language skills of our students. Students must draw upon interactional and personal functions of language while maintaining the group's cohesion. Norms, especially those that are co-constructed with students, encourage students to take responsibility for their behavior as well as their learning by allowing them to set the operational, process, and social-emotional conditions they need. Rather than list bad behaviors to be avoided, norms should describe the qualities students agree are necessary to create the learning environment they want. That's right: the norms of an SLC are themselves success criteria. They lay out how students will treat their fellow team members.

The norms that are developed by the entire class provide SLCs with a foundation for how members work together, even as specific SLC membership changes depending on the task or purpose. The development process begins, naturally, with an agreement of purpose. Let's look at how it typically takes shape with an illustration from Sophia Fericelli's 2nd grade classroom.

Ms. Fericelli begins by asking her students to think and talk with a partner or two about why it is important to have guidelines for the discussions they have in class. She listens in on the talk around her:

Lila: So everyone has a chance to talk.

Anthony: Yeah, you have to be polite.

Siobhan: And you have to talk about what you're supposed to talk about.

Ms. Fericelli then explains that they will be developing norms for their collaborative groups. She gives students a few minutes to write down as many ideas as they can think of and then share these ideas with the others in their groups. Students take turns reading one norm from their list. If the other students have that norm on their list, they put a check next to it; if they don't, they add it. By having each student read only one idea at a time rather than taking turns reading their entire list, Ms. Fericelli is able to make sure that all students have an opportunity to share.

When each group has a complete list, Ms. Fericelli asks them to share their ideas with the whole class. Each student draws a line under the last norm on their list and stands up in table groups. One group begins by reading their list aloud, again taking turns reading one item each so that all students are participating. Students in the other groups listen and repeat the prior process. If they hear an idea already on their list, it gets a check mark; if they hear a new idea, it gets added under a horizontal line they've drawn. Group by group, students stand up and read their list of suggested norms, with everyone else checking and adding.

With a list that now reflects all the ideas for discussion norms from all the groups, Ms. Fericelli explains that the class's next task is to come to consensus and prioritize the ideas to determine the top suggestions for norms. She writes the word *prioritize* on the board, pronounces it, and has the students repeat the word as a whole group and then to a partner. After a brief explanation of what it means to prioritize and how to do so, she models what this process looks like.

She projects her list on the document camera and reads the first two aloud:

> *Number 1: Listen when others are speaking. Number 2: Pay attention.* Hmm. I think these are really important, because if you don't listen to others, then you don't know what people are talking about and you can't join in the discussion. But listening and paying attention are really the same thing, so we don't need both of them. If you're *listening,* you have to be paying attention, so I'm going to cross out "Pay attention" and leave "Listen when others are speaking."

As the groups talk about the suggested norms, Ms. Fericelli walks around the room, giving assistance as needed. Then, as each group shares their top choices with the class, she writes them on a chart, adding a star next to each one when it is repeated by another group. Finally, she leads the class in a discussion to finalize the norms that will guide their group discussions. From this list she will create a rubric for self-assessment. She'll also remind groups of these norms before they begin SLC work. Periodically, she will ask them to assess their own participation in their groups.

———————————————

Older students probably don't need as much dedicated time to develop norms, but they can still benefit from spending some time discussing them. As an example, a common method for teaching point of view in the history class-room is through the use of debates, mock trials, and Socratic seminars. These arrangements all place a high demand on the academic discourse skills of the participants. Many teachers offer guidelines for successful participation in these exchanges and create rubrics for students to use to assess themselves. Guidelines are usually some variant on the following:

- Listen as an ally.
- Make connections to the comments of others.
- Pass if you don't have something to offer at that moment.
- Use accurate information to support your claims.
- Accept the questions of others in the spirit of learning.

Norms are more than a nice way to kick off collaborative learning. The fact is, they will emerge whether they are stated or not. Groups, just like nature, abhor a vacuum. In the absence of stated norms, informal ones invariably take hold as groups figure out how to work together (or not). The problem is that members' attitudes and dispositions, experiences, and knowledge work together to create a stew of psychological and procedural decisions that influence the group's effectiveness. Further, ineffective behaviors can become routinized over the course of the year and solidify unproductive techniques that become more difficult to displace.

Although norms relate directly to the work of groups, their construction benefits the individual. EL Education, a partnership between the Harvard Graduate School of Education and Outward Bound, notes that co-constructing norms gives students an opportunity for self-governance that "embodies the essence of self-discipline" (EL Education, n.d.). Importantly, as a teacher, your willingness to develop norms with students telegraphs vital messages about the learning environment. First, it alerts students to your expectations about their responsibility as members integral to the classroom community. Second, it provides you with an opportunity to discuss the characteristics of effective groups, as when Ms. Fericelli did a think-aloud focused on listening as a necessary condition. Claxton (2017) refers to the habits needed for collaboration as a student's learning power and defines them across four dispositions:

- **Resilience:** The ability to develop long-term goals, embrace challenge, and analyze errors.
- **Resourcefulness:** The ability to ask questions aligned with the purpose and challenge the status quo in an effort to innovate.
- **Reflection:** The ability to monitor one's own achievements in order to increase knowledge of self.
- **Relatedness:** The ability to learn, lead, and listen carefully with peers.

Norms are the ways groups function and are reflective of the dispositions they jointly possess. Individuals comprise the student learning community, and their own understanding of purposes and goals is crucial for them to arrive at shared agreements of success. Establishment of learning intentions and success criteria can provide SLCs with an initial pathway to establish their shared goals and build the dispositions they each need to propel learning.

Norms for virtual learning should similarly be co-constructed with students using the principles outlined above. Interactions in virtual spaces are comparatively new for students and their teachers, and norms have proven invaluable. One of the challenges many educators discovered when there was a rapid shift to online learning was that norms had not been established for this purpose. When considering norms for virtual interactions, keep these questions in mind:

- **Are students required to keep their cameras on during live interactions?** It's easy to immediately answer in the affirmative, but in practice, the issue may be more complicated. There may be bandwidth issues for the student's Wi-Fi, especially when there are multiple children in the home; turning off the camera may be a way to manage this. In addition, it may raise concerns in terms of cultural sensitivity, especially in maintaining the privacy of the family and the student. Not all students have access to a private space; they may need to be in a public part of the home. We recommend having private conversations with families to better understand and respond to their individual circumstances and needs.

- **How shall students log on to sessions?** You know the adage that "a stitch in time saves nine"? Keep in mind that children and adolescents don't always exhibit the best judgment in the moment. We recommend being proactive and developing a norm that students will always log on with their full name (not "Batman" or another non-identifier). In addition, we advise against allowing them to change their appearance (e.g., adding cat's ears or laser eyes). However, be sure to state your case for this norm in terms of the needs of the group rather than as (another) blanket rule. "Using your name makes it easier for everyone to address you correctly" is more useful than "No silly names."

- **How will groups gain your attention?** In a face-to-face classroom it is easy enough to raise a hand or even walk over to the teacher. But in virtual breakout rooms it may not be as intuitive. Teach your students how they can send you a message to request your presence in their small group virtual meeting. In addition, when students are working in their SLCs, make it a habit to pop into each virtual room. In the same way that you circulate in your physical classroom, you should be circulating in a virtual classroom. Students should anticipate that you will be a regular presence in their small groups.

Moving Forward . . .

Shared agreements about success are more than simply agreeing that the task is complete. Low-level compliance expectations do virtually nothing to build a student's sense of self, much less their academic prowess. Further, if the emphasis remains only on task completion, without proper attention to group and individual success criteria, students fail to calibrate what success looks like. Instead, they remain dependent on others, mostly the teacher, to tell them whether they learned something or not. Providing SLCs with the space to figure out their definitions of success given the task outcomes, to set goals and monitor their progress, and to continue to refine norms empowers learners. It's hard work for them, but it is well worth the investment.

Learning intentions and success criteria form the bookends of a lesson—the purpose and the learning destination. Articulating them is at the heart of teachers' clarity work. When done well, these criteria provide the teacher a clearer picture of his or her own lessons. They also furnish students with the language they need to learn with greater precision. For you, focusing students on learning intentions and success criteria requires instructional minutes, but they are minutes well spent. Rather than simply "pouring knowledge into students" (which doesn't work anyway), invest in developing a shared understanding of success with your students. Give them the opportunity to establish their own success criteria and monitor their own progress. In the process, you will develop a better understanding of your students and how they are making meaning of their learning.

The following questions are a good place to start, and you can use them going forward to monitor interactions in your classroom and inform your decisions relative to the shared agreements about success necessary for student learning communities to thrive.

1. Do your students know what they are supposed to learn in each lesson? How do you know?

2. Do your students know what success looks like, both individually and collectively? How do you know?

3. What type of goals do your students have for themselves? Are they performance and mastery? Are they individual and collective?

4. How might you teach students to monitor their progress?

5. What are the norms in your classroom? Did students help you construct them? How do these norms influence students' learning—particularly their collaborative learning?

Intentional
Collective Learning

Legendary UCLA basketball coach John Wooden was nearly as famous for his ability to mentor young people as he was for his unmatched winning record. His former players speak affectionately about their coach's maxims regarding success on and off the court: "Failing to prepare is preparing to fail." "Little things make big things happen." "It's what you learn after you know it all that counts." Above all, Coach Wooden understood that learning is continuous, and processing what has occurred is as important as the task itself. Yet this principle is often overlooked in classrooms during the rush to move on to the next unit of instruction. We might do well to heed Wooden's caution, "Be quick but don't hurry."

Effective educators, whether they are basketball coaches or biology teachers, teach with intention. They are able to view all the moving parts on the court or in the science lab, thinking strategically about ways to ensure that teams are functioning at optimal levels. Talented educators possess the ability to zoom in on an individual while simultaneously surveying the terrain to see whether progress is being made. They understand that teams learn—but only if these teams have the space to do so.

In addition, effective educators are intentional about how their teams are constructed. The grouping strategies they use aren't left to chance. Instead, they think carefully about how best to design deep collective learning so that every student profits academically and socially. They mix and reconstitute groups so that members bring out the best in one another.

When it comes to building student learning communities (SLCs), it is vital to ensure that members have an opportunity to examine their contributions and those of their groupmates. This is how groups get stronger. As noted in Chapter 4, SLCs need to have shared agreements of success and a game plan for achieving them. But they also need opportunities to devise ways to improve. Group members should discuss their progress and what they might do to increase their productivity or advance working relationships. This is a critical component of collective learning and one often neglected. This processing allows students to reflect on their actions and learning and to recommit to their studies.

Tim Halloran's 12th grade statistics students work in SLCs for the entire school year, and he requires that they "round table" after each unit of study. "I'm getting them ready for their college classes," he said, "and I know that next year they'll end up relying a lot on the cohesiveness of their study groups."

Mr. Halloran is currently teaching in a hybrid environment, with some days reserved for face-to-face instruction and other days dedicated to distance learning. As it turns out, his own recent learning experiences opened his eyes to related opportunities within this challenging situation:

> I went back to graduate school last year, and one of the things that surprised me was how much of our learning happened virtually. I also learned that although college freshmen and sophomores almost always have some distance learning courses, it's younger undergrads who are most likely to fail these courses—not because they don't know how to make the platform work, but because they don't possess the self-regulation skills they need when there isn't someone right in front of them.

Even as he focuses on helping his students learn and thrive right now, Mr. Halloran is seizing the chance to help better prepare his students for the distance learning they will face in college and career preparation programs. "I've learned how valuable it is to meet with my study group for my master's courses," he said. "Since we have to social distance in my physical classroom, I want to take advantage of developing these skills while I'm there to bridge their learning."

On the day before each major test, the SLCs spend about 15 minutes in their physical classroom discussing focus questions related to the ways they have worked together, which, according to Mr. Halloran, helps them "to notice their own learning and think about their contributions to the group." However, they accomplish this online. When they take the test the following day, they always find two questions related to their study habits within their virtual SLC. The first asks them to report the amount of time they spent studying alone or with the group outside class ("They're frightfully honest," Mr. Halloran said). The second asks them to estimate the grade they will receive on the test. Mr. Halloran explained:

> It's a good way for me to see how closely their estimations align with their performance. I want them to understand that math ability isn't something you're born with. It's a function of the amount of time and effort you put into it.

In this chapter, we address the metacognitive thinking of individuals and groups within the SLC process. These practices prompt reflective thinking and discussion, as well as group decision making. We'll also explore a number of ways groups can assess and communicate their progress—from practices as simple as writing down one thing the group did to encourage a member to participate or something a partner said that was encouraging, to rating how well the group used a targeted skill and identifying one thing the group could do better next time.

Team Cognition

The chief purpose of an SLC is to build and extend the knowledge and skills of its members. Sharing information is an important first step, but it's no guarantee that actual learning will occur; members need to actively acquire information from each other and make decisions about actions to take. But even as the *team's* knowledge pool grows, individual members are not going to benefit unless the group has ways to distribute unique information. Think of this another way: individuals possess some knowledge, skills, insights, or dispositions that are known only to themselves. However, knowledge that is privately held doesn't benefit the group. Groups need ways to disseminate knowledge internally, and every member needs to be receptive to learning from others in the SLC.

This type of interaction doesn't necessarily come naturally to students, and it can be limited further by students' communication skills. Fortunately, educators have developed a number of routines to facilitate knowledge distribution. One that's widely used and probably familiar to you is K-W-L (Ogle, 1986), a routine that poses three questions, each with a distinct purpose:

K   What do we **know?** (*Asked to solicit and disseminate both shared and unique knowledge*)

W   What do we **want** to know? (*Asked to arrive at shared agreements of success*)

L   What have we **learned?** (*Asked to promote reflection on learning*)

The K-W-L process is often a teacher-directed routine rather than a student-generated one, but there's no reason it has to be. "I've used K-W-L for years," 6th grade teacher Antonia Rollins told us, "but it only occurred to me this year that it could be a driver for my student learning communities." She explained that this inquiry process is ideal for helping students identify what they know about a problem and set their own goals. She shared an example of how, during a study of 20th century painters, one learner's K drove the rest of group's W in a whole new direction.

Each group began with individual members listing what they personally knew about the topic; then they recorded their collective knowledge on chart paper. When Marta mentioned Frida Kahlo, she drew blank looks from the rest of her team. "There's a big painting by her in my grandparents' house," Marta said. After searching for a few minutes on the Internet, she located it. "It's a self-portrait called *Me and My Parrots*," Marta explained, sharing her screen. "That's the artist and her four birds."

The other students in the group were intrigued by Kahlo's striking features (especially her eyebrows) and the cigarette she holds in one hand. And the conversation took a turn. "They realized that nearly all the artists they had listed were white men, such as Andy Warhol and Pablo Picasso," Ms. Rollins said. "They asked themselves, what did they know about *female* artists of the 20th century, about *artists of color?* And they began shaping their learning goals to reflect the wonderings Marta had sparked."

Team Metacognition

Deep collective learning gives students opportunities not only to consolidate and expand academic knowledge but also to gain a greater understanding of themselves as learners *and* as a member of a community of learners.

As teachers we know about *metacognition,* thinking about thinking, the ability to perceive one's one learning (Flavell, 1979). A key element of metacognition is the ability to plan and then execute the plan; this typically develops over time, beginning in early childhood and continuing through adolescence. It happens that student learning communities are a great environment for building individuals' awareness of how they think, how they learn, and under which circumstances they think and learn best. This can be fostered through tasks that encourage groups to establish goals and assign roles to reach those goals, as discussed in Chapter 4.

The definition of metacognition has evolved over the years. Whereas once it was focused on a person's ability to use declarative knowledge, metacognition is now understood to also include memory, attention, and a *theory of mind* (Perner, 1991), which is an awareness that thoughts, ideas, and perceptions vary across people. Developing a theory of mind means we come to understand that our thinking can be different from the thinking of others.

Most of us have seen very young children "hide" by covering their eyes—*if I can't see you, then you can't see me, because what I see is the same thing you see.* It takes years for young children to develop a theory of mind and its attending empathetic and social skills. The first step is when they begin to differentiate themselves from their mothers, exhibit joint attention to an object (as when being read to), and point at something to direct another person's attention. Only at around 3 to 4 years of age do children begin to demonstrate an understanding that others have a different view of the world than they themselves do. In the years that follow, the development of empathy and perspective taking can be encouraged through exposure to the thoughts and feelings of others, especially through experiences that foster perception of differing points of view.

Perceiving others' thinking requires a command of the vocabulary to describe it. Kindergartners are developing a vocabulary of metacognition related to the perspectives of others, such as *teach, learn, remember,* and *forget.* Most children at this age are able to determine accurately when someone else is doing these things. However, they have more difficulty with the metacognitive vocabulary of words such as *guess, wonder,* and *figure out,* because these mental actions are less readily apparent to others (Lockl & Schneider, 2006). There is emerging evidence that a reader's development of a theory of mind is linked to reading comprehension, as a perception of character's emotional and mental states is essential to understanding narrative text structures (Dore, Amendum, Golinkoff, & Hirsh-Pasek, 2018).

Teachers' support for metacognitive development can boost SLC effectiveness. One way that kindergarten teacher Ana Mendoza does this is by teaching and using mental-state verbs with her class. "We call them *thinking words*," she explained, pointing out how they are grouped on her word wall. In addition to the words previously mentioned, she features others: *hope, wish, want, feel, decide, imagine, prefer, notice,* and *believe.* "I ask questions about these words when we read about characters in stories," Ms. Mendoza told us. "I want to build my students' ability to see that other people sometimes think differently from them. It helps in their SLCs, too."

Ms. Mendoza said the book *The Day the Crayons Quit* (Daywalt, 2013) is a help in this effort. "The crayons are all arguing with each other, so they bring their own perspectives. Then there's Duncan, the boy who is trying to make sense of what each of them is saying," she explained. As one example of the many conflicts in the book, Red Crayon asserts that he is tired and overworked because he is used so much in holiday pictures. Here, Ms. Mendoza pauses to ask her students some key questions: "What is Red Crayon noticing? How do you know?" and "What would Red Crayon prefer? Why do you think so?"

Later in the story, Duncan tries a solution that will satisfy many of the crayons, at least to some extent. As her students analyze the picture Duncan drew, Ms. Mendoza asks further questions that challenge them to move between the boy's thinking and the Red Crayon's perceptions: "What were the problems that Duncan was trying to figure out? Will all of Red Crayon's wishes be solved by Duncan's solution? What would Red Crayon imagine to be a better solution than Duncan's?"

Why these questions? Ms. Mendoza explained:

> As much as I am able, I try to get them to consider what others are thinking, not just their own thoughts. I also have a few question stems for accountable talk that use these thinking words. I keep them on table tents so the kids can see them. Getting insight into what others think comes with age and experience, but there's no reason it can't begin right here in this classroom.

Team Reflection

Student learning communities benefit from group processes that provide time to debrief tasks once completed. This is different from the progress monitoring discussed in Chapter 4, which is chiefly done incrementally throughout the task. Post-task reflection allows teams to note their collective efforts as well as individual contributions. Whereas progress monitoring is reflection *in* action, post-task debriefs are reflections *on* action (Schön, 1983). It's a way for SLCs to identify areas of strength and opportunities for growth in future collaborations.

This kind of purposeful group processing has a metacognitive component. To engage fully, members must first think about what they have learned personally from the task, reflecting on the new knowledge and skills they acquired as individuals as well as the behaviors they employed. The ability to notice one's own learning and behavior is central to reflective discussion. Further, self-knowledge is linked to transfer of skills from one setting to another (Billing, 2007). Post-task self-reflections begin with evaluating one's progress against goals, recognizing the problem-solving skills enlisted during the task, and reporting behaviors that helped or hindered one's learning.

Although these behaviors sound complex, in truth, they can be simplified to meet the developmental needs of the students involved. For example, a primary student might respond to a series of smiling and frowning faces, whereas an older student might use a Likert-type scale (1–5) to evaluate progress (see Figure 5.1).

FIGURE 5.1

Team Reflection Questions

For younger students . . .	For older students . . .
I reached my learning goal today.	I set a learning goal for myself in this group and I reached it. (not yet) 1 2 3 4 5 (definitely)
I helped myself to be a learner.	When I was confused about something, I asked my team or the teacher. (not yet) 1 2 3 4 5 (definitely)
I helped someone else learn.	I provided ideas that my team could use. (not yet) 1 2 3 4 5 (definitely)

Teachers of secondary students can add open-ended questions like these:

- What contributions did I make?
- What additional contributions could I have made?
- What is an example of when I worked well in our group?
- What is one thing that I could have done better?

Open-ended questions are a good way to prompt students to reflect on the behavioral elements of learning, including study habits, effort, and use of human and text-based resources. Combined with closed-response questions, they can illuminate important habits of mind for both teacher and student.

These self-reflection questionnaires also provide a basis for team reflection, although we want to stress that we are not fans of team reflections that require members to rate or evaluate one another. Doug calls these "rat out your friends" forms, and that's not what we're advocating. Instead, students should focus their reflections on their contributions to the group. It is also important to remember that elementary students are not necessarily equipped to reflect deeply as a team without a good deal of support. True reflection is more than simply cataloging the sequence of steps followed or chronicling the failures of others—and both of these made to be made clear for younger students.

One more thing to keep in mind: not all tasks automatically translate to learning. Most of us can recall a science lab experiment, a field trip, or a project we designed that kept students busy but didn't deepen their learning. The metaphor of a painting and a frame has been used to describe the relationship between an *experience* and a *reflection* (Boud, Keogh, & Walker, 2013). The experience is much like a painting; the frame (the reflection) brings the boundaries and contours of the experience into a sharper focus. Reflecting on an experience can reframe that experience by turning it into learning, but the skill of reflection needs to be taught.

We have found success in a five-stage process to scaffold the team reflection process that is based on Moon's (2004) levels of reflection. The first step is **noticing** what occurred, and the second is **making sense** of what occurred. These early steps aren't going to yield much in the way of reflective thinking, but they are necessary to organize thinking. The third step is **making meaning,** and at this point the team is asked to entertain what was surprising and why it may have happened (which is one of the knowledge emotions discussed in Chapter 3). The fourth step is a crucial one, as the team is asked to **work with meaning** by considering what actions members want to take next time.

This is important to prevent members of a team from blaming one another and encourage them to consider instead how their experience might inform future decisions. The fifth step is **transformational learning,** as the group is asked to consider how its members have changed (learned) as a result of the experience.

In order for students to become proficient collaborative learners, they need opportunities to practice and then reflect on what worked and what needs to be improved. Seventh grade science teacher Elijah Hill uses a team reflection process whenever his SLCs engage in longer projects. Because he views teaching students the importance and value of examining group behaviors as a process that requires support, he models the reflective frame for them over the course of several weeks before handing the responsibility off to them.

When we visited Mr. Hill's classroom, students were using the reflection process but still receiving plenty of targeted support. During a science investigation on environmental issues, Mr. Hill moved among the SLCs, noting interactions, comments, and group behaviors for them to draw on later. When the projects were complete, he asked his students to reflect first on their own learning, and then on the learning of their SLC. "The first rule is that their written reflection should take me no more than 30 seconds to read," he said. "I want them to be concise." He also explained that he wants his students to realize that, even when they achieve their learning goals, "It doesn't mean there's nothing more to learn."

One of Mr. Hill's SLCs investigated honeybee colony collapse disorder, and they were mostly successful in achieving their goals (see Figure 5.2). "They did a really good job," Mr. Hill said. He elaborated:

> I was really pleased with what their team came up with. They earned an A– on the project, and they didn't even talk about the grade! They recognized that they got stuck early on because they wanted to start Googling stuff without really having a plan. I met with them on Tuesday and asked them some questions about how they were organizing what they were learning. They ended up having to retrace their steps. Seems like they saw that slowed them down.

Best Practices for Composing SLCs

We have intentionally delayed addressing issues related to group formation until this point, because we want to disrupt conventional thinking of grouping as a purely social function.

FIGURE 5.2

Reflective Team Thinking

Levels of reflection	SLC reflective thinking
Level 1: Noticing *What was your assignment? What work did you do?*	We completed an investigation on honeybee colony collapse throughout the world. We were able to gather information from several sources and we completed a report and presentation for the class.
Level 2: Making sense *Did you have the information or skills needed?*	We relied on information from an NPR report to get us started. We found a report from the EPA that helped. One problem we had was organizing the information in a spreadsheet. It slowed us up at first.
Level 3: Making meaning *Why did (or didn't) it happen? Did anything surprise you?*	We didn't take enough time to figure out how we were all going to enter info in the document and then it got to be a mess pretty quick. We ended up having to redo some of our early research because we didn't capture the right info.
Level 4: Working with meaning *What should you do next time?*	Next time we need to have more organization from the beginning. Some people were reading the same sources and then it was duplicated. We didn't have a place to write source info and then we had to go find it again.
Level 5: Transformational learning *How have your assumptions, understandings, and future actions been shaped by this experience?*	Mr. Hill likes to say that sometimes you have to go slow to go fast. Next time we need to take more time to plan out how we're going to do the investigation and set up the spreadsheet so we can all make sense of it. We realized that if other people can't understand the notes it is a waste of time.

As when composing any other high-performing team, SLC formation must be predicated on the purpose (task) and goals (success criteria). The social aspects of groups are very much in play but are strongly influenced by supportive relational conditions (see Chapter 3). Every teacher has been guilty at some point of taking students "as is" and trying to put together groups. This relegates teachers to the role of matchmaker, trying to come up with the right alchemy. It's a practice that generally results in two effective groups at best, with the rest muddling along and one flaming out altogether. Then, when the next task comes along, it's a matter of mixing things up and hoping (fingers crossed) that *this time,* all the lineups will be winning ones. Breaking this frustrating cycle calls for a more deliberate approach based on a few solid principles.

Create Mixed-Ability Groups

The subject of grouping has been hotly debated by teachers and intensely studied by researchers interested in achievement and social growth. The findings point to widespread agreement that mixed-ability (*heterogeneous*) grouping during collaborative learning produces the best results for students academically and emotionally.

Although there may be a certain surface logic to separating students in ability-alike (*homogeneous*) groups, the only students who see even a small positive effect from this arrangement are high-achieving ones. Average-achieving students see more benefit from mixed-ability grouping (Lou et al., 1996; Nurenberg, 2016), and there is a large body of research documenting how homogeneous grouping suppresses the achievement levels of struggling learners (e.g., Meijnen & Guldemond, 2002). Not only does ability-alike grouping not seem to result in increased achievement, but it can be harmful to students' self-esteem and self-efficacy (see Corwin Visible Learning, 2019; Hattie, 2019a, 2019b; Oakes, 2005), which may further inhibit school success. Given that structural inequalities in our society perpetuate a legacy of low achievement for some learners (Hill, 2017), homogeneous grouping demands scrutiny from an equity perspective. To what extent does it reinforce variable expectations and opportunities to learn (Garrett & Hong, 2016)? At a time when educators are rightfully addressing inequity at the district and school levels, we must not miss the problematic classroom practices that are right in front of us.

Grouping students into ability-alike homogeneous teams also runs counter to evidence on the effectiveness of teams. Groups are, on average, smarter than any single member. As Surowiecki (2005) noted in his book *The Wisdom of Crowds,* "Under the right circumstances, groups are remarkably intelligent, and are often smarter than the smartest people in them" (p. xiii). Under the right conditions, group members educate one another through interaction. Members share information and experiences, thus building one another's background knowledge.

This is not to say that students should never be grouped by skill development or instructional need. When a teacher is there to guide instruction—and we mean *physically or virtually present* with the learners in the group—it makes sense to have students who have similar needs work together. However, when it comes to student-led teams, ability-alike grouping is often detrimental to lower-achieving students. Because SLCs are, by nature, student-led and not teacher-directed, their functionality depends on the full range of the cognitive, metacognitive, and relational resources its members bring. The conclusion? SLCs should be heterogeneous, full stop.

They should also be mindfully structured, as the composition of a group plays a factor in its relative success. Bennett and Cass (1989) looked at the performance of groups where either the high-achieving students outnumbered the low-achieving ones, or vice versa. They found that when groups were structured so that the number of high-achieving students outnumbered those who were lower achieving, the tendency was for the majority to take control of the task and complete it with little regard to the learning of members who need more time and repetition. Bennett and Cass also found that when groups were structured at a ratio of one high-achieving student for every two lower-achieving ones, the result was more discussion and learning for all members. They concluded that groups that were dominated by high-achieving students performed worse *because* the low-achieving student was left out of the process. Although this exact formula—two low-achieving students for every one high-achiever—may not be feasible for every classroom, it is worth noting as a reminder not to inadvertently set up groups willing to leave a learner behind, as everyone in these groups will wind up for the worse.

If you ask students if they enjoy working in mixed-ability groups, they usually say yes—and even that they prefer it. They certainly do in elementary school (Elbaum, Schumm, & Vaughn, 1997) and middle school (Tereshchenko et al., 2019). Students identified as talented and gifted in grades 5–11 acknowledge the social development benefits that result from working in heterogeneous groups (Adams-Byers, Whitsell, & Moon, 2004). One lesson we have learned from implementing SLCs with mixed-ability groups is this: when collaboration with peers becomes a routine part of the learning rather than an anomaly, students settle into a pattern of work that is productive without being disruptive.

In addition, we want to remind you that groups thrive only when they have the relational conditions they need to thrive. Teachers must be sure to teach and model the necessary language and social skills. In her study of homogeneous and heterogeneous collaborative learning groups in 6th grade mathematics, Leonard (2001) found that *group cohesiveness* (working toward a mutually accepted goal) was the critical factor in the participation and learning for both high- and low-achieving students.

Group Flexibly with Cognitive Variables in Mind

Leonard's findings and the work of other researchers remind us that the magic of group learning comes as much from the skills of the collective group as from the skills of individual members.

Flexible grouping allows students to work with many classmates over time, build relationships, and broaden their learning experiences. SLCs are not static, and an outcome of SLCs should be to build the capacity of all students to work with a large network of people. After all, the workplace is rarely a homogeneous environment—adults are called upon daily to interact and work with people who possess a range of strengths and areas of need. Flexible grouping patterns (Flood, Lapp, Flood, & Nagel, 1992) can be based on many different variables beyond current academic performance and specific to the students in classroom. Here are a number to consider:

- **Interest.** Students are grouped together to study a topic of interest or spread among groups to serve as motivators.
- **Work habits.** Students are spread among groups to model dispositions and organizational skills.
- **Prior knowledge of content.** Students are spread among groups to share topical knowledge.
- **Task.** Students are grouped together because the purpose of the task has been designed to meet their needs.
- **Social.** Students are spread among groups to serve as leaders or in other specialized roles.

With group cohesiveness and specific tasks in mind, we often use an *alternate ranking system* to formulate groups. We compose a list of students in rank order of their academic, organizational, and social skills, yielding a cumulative overall score. For example, in a 30-student classroom, a student may rank as 1 in academic skills, a 6 in organizational skills, but 21 in social skills, for an overall score of 28. Using the overall scores, we rank-order students from highest to lowest and divide the list in two equal portions. For instance, students ranked 1 through 15 would be on the first list, and students ranked 16 through 30 on the second. We then compose groups by partnering student 1 with student 16, student 2 with student 17, as so on. This gives us partners who are heterogeneous yet not so far apart that they have difficulty bridging the divide. Although not completely foolproof, this approach provides a starting point for creating groups systematically.

Angel Bautista created a list of his 30 high school science students in order of their academic performance on a recent formative assessment, as well as his observations of previous work in the SLCs (especially their organizational and communication skills). Brandi received the highest cumulative score, followed by Jenna (see Figure 5.3). In the middle, number 15, was Raquel. Araceli (originally number 17) and Jenna were not currently speaking, so it didn't make sense to put them in a group together following our alternate ranking system approach. Mr. Bautista decided to swap positions 17 and 18, adding Araceli to a different group. In the end, some SLCs had more members than others. Mr. Bautista explained his process:

> I made a few adjustments based on some things I've learned about individual students. I added an extra member, Juliette, to one team because I've seen these students in action in other teams, and because they're strong, I'd like to stretch them to expand their collaborative skills. I also have a student who came in at the middle of the year after homeschooling for most of his school career. He hasn't had a lot of experience working with peers, so I want to give him a little more space to adjust. I'll also be checking in with that SLC more often to see how it's going.

FIGURE 5.3

Using Alternate Ranking to Form SLCs

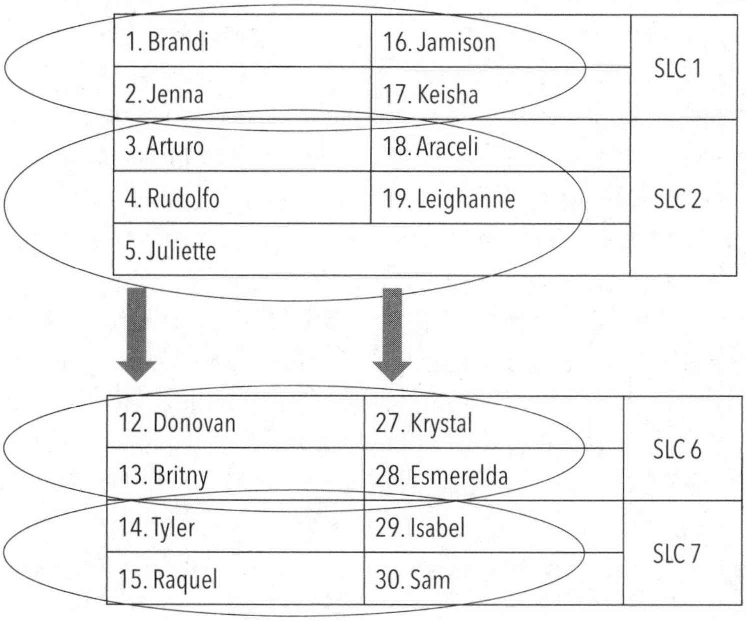

Be Deliberate About Group Size and Duration

In Chapter 3, we shared a couple of different examples of students working in groups of four to six. When the question is group size, a good rule of thumb is to favor partners or triads for the primary grades and groups of four or more for students in grades 4 and above. Not every class roster will divide conveniently into these numbers, so a little variation is fine. As with Doug and Nancy's student Tarik (see Chapter 3), some students benefit from a slightly smaller team size. So, in your physical or virtual classroom, there might be a group or two of five students and a group consisting of three students. Or there might be a couple students working in partner pairs and the rest working in groups of three or four.

We recommend capping group size at five. Our experience suggests that when groups get to be six or bigger, the risk of leaving a student out increases. In a virtual setting, larger groups become a reason for some members to go silent and allow others to carry the discussion. Some tend to be excluded from full participation in the discourse. Fay, Garrod, and Carletta (2000) found that, when group size was 10, "communication is like monologue and members are influenced most by the dominant speaker" (p. 481). That's clearly not what we want. Try to keep your group size small enough to ensure that every student benefits from all that deep collective learning can offer.

Another reason to keep group sizes relatively small is to reduce social loafing, which is an individual's reduced effort during a collaborative task. There is a fair amount of this that happens in any group, regardless of the age, medium, or expertise of participants. Larger groups tend to have a higher degree of social loafing, and small groups experience less free riding. Habitual social loafers earn a reputation among their peers and create higher levels of frustration in their team. By and large, smaller groups tend to be more organized and effective (Arterberry, Cain, & Chopko, 2007).

The amount of time your lesson plan allots for a task should also factor into the size of the team. Generally speaking, the longer the duration of the task, the larger the group might be. A group of four students might struggle to complete a five-minute task, for example, because there isn't enough time for all to contribute. However, long projects (especially those that continue for a week or more) are fine for groups of four or five because there are more opportunities for interaction and contribution.

We tend to keep SLCs together for about six weeks to allow the team to develop optimal working relationships, strong communication patterns, and social cohesion. This is an important consideration in a distance learning environment, where it may take a bit longer for groups to find their groove academically and emotionally. At the beginning of the school year, you may want to keep groups together for a shorter period of time (two weeks or so) until you have had an opportunity to get to know your students better and identify their strengths and opportunities for growth. If you are teaching at a distance, it is essential that you are regularly participating in their discussions so you can gather the observational data you need for composing future SLCs.

Have a Plan for When a Group Doesn't Work

What about when a group doesn't work? As we noted in Chapter 1, sometimes groups don't complete their tasks, or one member does all the work, or they divide and attempt to conquer the task. The first thing to determine is whether the difficulty is related to a specific episode, such as a disagreement about the task. If that is the case, the best approach is to assist the team in reaching a decision. In other cases, the task itself may be causing the problem. If so, consider your instructional design. The group may not be ready for the task, which means you need to do some more guided instruction. If this proves insufficient, assume more of the cognitive responsibility and model, model, model.

In rare cases, the root cause of the difficulty may be a personality mismatch between students. Assist the group in repairing relationships and monitor closely so that you can offer continuity during disruptive intervals. If the problem proves to be intractable, consider reconstituting the groups and provide additional support to students who are having trouble with the interpersonal skills required. These students might need some additional scaffolds, such as task cards or a checklist of items to do. Above all, resist the urge to allow a student to work alone. Although it may be the easy way out, it deprives that student of the opportunity to learn the necessary habits needed in an SLC.

A Checklist for Intentional Collective Learning

SLCs are only able to flourish when they are intentionally built, maintained, and refined. Without intention on the part of the teacher, the teams that emerge are inconsistent and inequitable. Figure 5.4 provides a list of questions for planning, designing, evaluating, and troubleshooting SLCs, inspired by the work of Barbara Gross Davis (1993). We encourage you to use these as a guide in your work to help these teams take hold in your classroom.

FIGURE 5.4

Planning, Designing, Evaluating, and Troubleshooting SLCs

Component	Questions to consider
Preparing students to work in groups	• Are there general skills students need to learn and practice in order to work collaboratively in groups regardless of the task (e.g., active listening, helping one another master content, giving and receiving constructive criticism, managing disagreements)? • How and when will you teach them these skills? • What are the biggest stumbling blocks for students getting started, and how will you help them overcome those obstacles?
Designing group work	• Do your group tasks require interdependence, in which students are responsible to and dependent on others in the group? • Is there a fair division of labor for each member? • What kinds of rewards or encouragement will you use to support or motivate students working in groups? • Are group tasks differentiated to ensure students are working toward the standard, while accounting for differences in language or literacy skills? • How will students support peers in their group who struggle due to language or learning differences? • Will you use competitions or category winners? • Do students have opportunities to work together face-to-face as well as online?
Organizing learning groups	• How will you compose student groups? For example, do you need to accommodate large numbers of English learners? Are there students whose social skills need careful consideration? • Is there an optimal size for groups? • How will you help groups to devise a plan of action (who will be doing what and when)? • How will decisions be made within the group? • For tasks or projects that span a number of days or weeks, what processes will you use to check progress? • How will students deal with uncooperative members or manage conflicts?
Evaluating group work	• How will group work be evaluated (i.e., by you, by the group, by individuals within the group)? • Does the evaluation include both the quality of the product and the effectiveness of the group? • How will you communicate the grading system to students? • If some group work will not be formally evaluated, what kinds of feedback will be offered instead? • After working in groups, how do students' perceptions and feelings about group work change?
Dealing with student concerns	• How will you assess students' feelings about working in groups? Do you know about their prior experiences with group work and whether those experiences were positive or negative? • How will you encourage students who would rather work alone to participate? • What signs might you look for to determine that a group is not working out? What actions can you take when you notice this?

Moving Forward . . .

Have you come across and read an old diary of yours? Or looked back through your high school yearbook, shaking your head at the comments of your peers? If you are like most people, these trips down memory lane are a reminder of how far you've traveled. The distance between who you were then and who you are now was gained through the choices you've made and the experiences you've had. As educators, it is important that all of us regularly stop, step back, and take stock of our work. Reflecting on where we are, where we want to be, and what it will take to get there helps us grow as professionals. And the evidence of our growth is usually sitting right in front of us, five days a week: our students.

Our students also have much to learn by looking back at their work and interactions and by talking about what worked and what didn't. It allows them to plan for what to do differently the next time in order to improve their collective effectiveness. Team processing can open the door to academic and social growth, and teachers hold the key. Giving students time do this will enhance their metacognitive powers and make them stronger learners.

The following questions are a good place to start, and you can use them going forward to monitor interactions in your face-to-face or virtual classroom and inform your decisions relative to the intentional collective learning necessary for student learning communities to thrive.

1. How have you taught and monitored team cognition and team metacognition?

2. What opportunities do your students have to reflect on their experiences in student learning communities? What do these reflections tell you about your students?

3. How do you typically form groups, and do these groups function as student learning communities? What might you change about your grouping going forward?

4. How can you respond when groups struggle to be successful?

Peer Supports
That Amplify Learning

Feedback provides information about how one is progressing toward a goal—and it's everywhere. If you are walking down the street and someone walking in front of you makes an extraordinary effort to avoid something in their path, that's feedback. You use it to either adjust or prepare to adjust your own journey. At the very least, you are more cautious, alert to factors that might merit consideration or potential obstacles in your way. In short, this feedback provided by someone walking along the same path you are gives you important information to make your journey more successful. The same principle applies in student learning communities. Effective peer-to-peer feedback provides the necessary support for the success of collective learning.

Christen Wenger is a 3rd grade teacher who uses peer support in her virtual classroom during mathematics. "My learners benefit more when they support each other," she explained. "They are more likely to take what they hear from their peers and put it to use not only in their problem solving but also in other areas, like writing." Let's see how this works.

───────────────

This morning in Ms. Wenger's distance learning classroom, learners are working with equivalent fractions within the context of perimeter.

Her students are learning from home, and the children have their own math manipulatives supplied by the school, including fraction tiles, fraction circles, fraction towers, and pieces of different-colored construction paper. Within their groups, they are addressing an anchor problem: "The perimeter of the rectangle is 17½ feet. If the length is 6⅓ feet, what is the length of the other sides?"

> **Zavian:** We have to make those fractions improper.
>
> **Alexis:** Wait . . . I have this wrong, I think. We can't just subtract the length from the perimeter?
>
> **Christina:** [Holding up fraction circles to the camera] Look—they have different bottom numbers, and that won't work, see?
>
> **Zavian:** [Pointing to his fraction circles] The bottom number is called the denominator, Christina. That's what we're supposed to call it. And we have to make these fractions improper so that we can work with them.

If we take a step back from this scenario, we can notice several important things happening in this student learning community:

- Zavian, Alexis, and Christina are all actively engaged in the task.
- They are interacting socially in a way that supports their learning—talking about the mathematical concepts that factor in the problem and investing in the effort.
- They have a shared agreement on success: *Find the other sides of the rectangle.*
- Solving this problem is a means through which these learners are intentionally working on their cognitive regulation and social skills.

The support offered to Alexis is particularly interesting. Notice how Zavian and Christina contributed in ways that amplified her learning. Let's see what happens next as the group presses on.

Drawing on the guidance from her peers, Alexis begins using the fraction circles to find a common denominator. She thinks aloud:

I think that the common denominator is 6, see? When you use the sixths pieces, we can find the common denominator for ½ and ⅓. So let's do what Zavian said and convert to improper fractions. Christina, can you draw this out on the construction paper and hold it up to your camera so that we can keep track of our numbers? Zavian, I am going to try and convert these fractions to improper fractions. Will you help me?

The learners in Ms. Wenger's online classroom regularly support each other in their SLCs. The exchange between these three learners illustrates rich peer support in the form of feedback. This isn't just any feedback, however, with students simply telling their peers they are wrong or offering empty platitudes. The type of feedback Zavian and Christina provided helped Alexis focus on the shared agreement of success, provided insight into where the team is in its progression toward success, and helped the team decide where to go next. To get to this point, each of these students needed to have the self-efficacy to seek help, the prosocial skills to contribute to their fellow team members' success, and the ability to navigate the necessary communication channels to relay this peer-to-peer support. The opportunities this task gave them to use these skills helped them develop those competencies further. In this chapter, we'll look at how the peer support of SLCs amplifies members' learning.

The Skill of Seeking Help

Ms. Wenger's students understand that the day's learning links them together as a collaborative team; they cannot individually meet the success criteria for the learning experience or task unless they all meet the success criteria. Zavian, Alexis, and Christina knew they needed to synchronize their efforts in tackling the perimeter problem. If one learner were out of step with fellow team members, they would be unlikely to meet both individual and team success criteria. As Ms. Wenger put it, "If you have four students sitting together but working independently, the group will not work."

Positive interdependence—the idea that every member of the collaborative team is needed to meet the day's learning intentions and success criteria—is facilitated by both individual and group accountability. Ms.

Wenger explained, "Whether in math, writing, or science, I make sure there are timelines, multiple individual and group check-ins, and opportunities for my students to evaluate themselves and their group's progress. I have these on my LMS, and I build in these check-ins during my live sessions." She has a clear system to help her learners understand that they are linked together in this experience or task, and she has found that "making sure they are accountable for themselves and as a group has really increased their willingness to seek help from their peers and, in any way possible, support their peers when they can." Ms. Wenger has been able to promote positive interdependence within her collaborative learning teams so that her students recognize and embrace their role in their team's collective learning. She also provides measures of accountability for making progress toward the agreed-upon success criteria, which ensures that her students can clearly identify their contribution and recognize when they must seek support from their fellow team members (Johnson & Johnson, 1990).

For peers to support peers, members of the collaborative team must be able to recognize when they need help and then bring that need to the team in the form of promotive interaction. *Promotive interaction* is the willingness of the team to facilitate one another's contributions through peer-to-peer support. Remember how Alexis indicated to the others that she needed assistance with the perimeter problem? She recognized that there was likely something wrong with her first solution approach and did not hesitate to make that realization visible to the group.

Let's look at another example. Jackson, a 4th grader, was struggling with the difference between a simile and a metaphor, and this was preventing him from moving forward in the writing component of his team's design-based task in science. Like Alexis, Jackson knew he had to seek help because successfully completing his component of the task was necessary for the collective learning of the SLC. He also knew that his team was there to support him. So he just asked for help: "Can you all help me figure out the difference between a simile and a metaphor?" This question kicked off a round of academic discourse that not only clarified the concept for Jackson such that he could carry out his part of the task but also enhanced the entire team's overall understanding of these two types of figurative language. Peers supported peers, and collective learning resulted.

When every member of an SLC is comfortable seeking help from fellow team members, learners develop an awareness of what others do not understand and what they themselves have to offer. When they leverage their individual skills, expertise, and background knowledge to help one another, they also help themselves. Zavian and Christina and Jackson's peers all benefit from these opportunities to retrieve the information from their own minds, enhancing their knowledge of the content, skills, and understandings linked to the experience or task (Webb & Mastergeorge, 2003).

The skill of seeking help is knowing what to do when you don't know what to do. It develops in, and through, SLCs when the following conditions are met:

1. Each team member knows their peers are willing to provide support when it is needed.

2. There is a clear and embraced expectation that team members will share the necessary resources.

3. Individual team members seek support knowing that others will challenge their thinking and reasoning for the collective good of the team.

4. All members of the team can work constructively with one another.

SLCs thrive on trust, generosity, openness, and cooperation. If a team lacks any of these, there's is a greater likelihood that individual members will look to outside assistance (the teacher) when they meet an obstacle. Imagine, too, if Alexis's or Jackson's admissions of struggle had been met with ridicule, exasperation, or shaming. How likely would they be to ask their peers for support the next time they found themselves struggling with a task or a concept? Ms. Wenger shared some particularly valuable insight on this point:

> When individual students ask me for help on group projects, I ask them if they have met with their teammates. If they say no or indicate that they don't want to ask their group members, I know I need to reevaluate the makeup of that particular team. Something is not working.

The Prosocial Skills of Peer Support

Having spent so much of this book sharing examples of successful SLCs operating in other teachers' classroom, we thought we'd approach the second key aspect of building peer support capacity by sharing a less successful example from one of our own classrooms.

When John taught high school mathematics, he worked hard to engage his learners as mathematicians. In algebra, for example, the learning intentions he set were focused on students justifying, explaining, and supporting their approach to a particular problem. Whether they were solving a system of linear inequalities or developing a mathematical model for a particular phenomenon, John wanted his learners to wrestle with mathematical ideas through mathematical discourse.

That's what he *wanted,* anyway. As an early-career teacher, he saw that it rarely played out like this in his classroom. He put learners together into groups, provided them with an authentic scenario, and then asked them to come up with a solution and prepare a mathematical justification for their approach. What typically resulted was a lot of bickering and fighting—and disengaged learners. Through his conferencing with students, John knew they could justify, explain, and support their mathematical thinking. However, when they were placed in collaborative learning teams, the situation quickly devolved into chaos. What John now knows is that, although his students' academic skills were properly suited to the challenge, they didn't have the prosocial stills they needed to tackle this work in a group setting. They didn't know how to work with and support their peers, and he didn't identify this as a necessary instructional target.

John's experience is a common one. Collective learning teams can devolve into compliance, disengagement, resistance, and rebellion because individual members lack the interpersonal skills required to engage in critical conversations or dialogue around a learning experience or task. If learners do not have experience applying specific interpersonal skills to a collaborative learning environment, there will be a breakdown in the group's positive interdependence as well as its promotive interaction. They will not see the value their peers bring to the experience or task, and they will not seek to encourage or support them in the learning. In short, for collective learning to work, prosocial skills need to be explicitly negotiated in the form of norms (see Chapter 3), and, if necessary, they need to be taught using the gradual release of responsibility framework (Fisher & Frey, 2014). Figure 6.1 lists common prosocial skills that support collaborative learning and the subskills needed to successfully apply them in face-to-face and virtual environments.

The key message here is that you cannot take for granted that your learners will be equipped to support one another in a way that ensures deep collective learning. Again, these skills must be negotiated and often explicitly taught.

FIGURE 6.1

Prosocial Skills for Student Learning Communities

Prosocial skill	Subskills
Leadership	• Offers guidance and organizational suggestions in order for group to complete task • Allows others to voice opinions and assume responsibilities • Shares in successes and failures • Encourages the group to move toward the goal
Decision making	• Listens to the opinions of others and takes these into consideration • Identifies possible courses of action and accurately describes the costs and benefits of each • Is willing to make a choice when the group needs to come to a decision
Trust building	• Follows through on commitments to others • Contributes to a positive atmosphere • Disagrees respectfully • Accurately assesses own competence
Turn taking	• Listens when others are talking and does not interrupt • Acknowledges others who have spoken • Makes sure everyone is included • Offers supportive statements • Uses verbal and nonverbal signals to invite responses from others
Active listening	• Makes eye contact with the speaker • Uses an open posture • Stops other activities to listen • Paraphrases statements of others • Asks clarifying questions • Seeks and offers feedback
Conflict management	• Listens to the opinions of others and takes these into consideration • Avoids hurtful statements about others • States own views without becoming defensive • Is able to identify the concerns of self and others • Accepts the group's decision graciously • Is able to resume the task

Source: From *Productive Group Work* (p. 70), by D. Fisher, N. Frey, and S. Everlove, 2009, Alexandria, VA: ASCD. Copyright 2009 by ASCD.

The benefit of explicit instruction of prosocial skills far outweighs the instructional time commitment. Research tells us that when learners receive explicit instruction in the prosocial skills essential for cooperation, they are more inclusive in their cooperative efforts with peers, more respectful and considerate of the value their peers bring to the group, and more detailed in the explanations they provide to support the learning of their peers (Durlak, Weissberg, Dymnicki, Taylor, & Schellinger, 2011; Gillies & Ashman, 1996, 1998). These findings bring us back to our earlier discussion of positive interdependence and promotive interactions. When teachers take these prosocial behaviors seriously, and when we make them an integral part of our classroom environment rather than an afterthought, we set the stage for effective peer support.

Our role as teachers includes teaching prosocial skills and providing well-designed experiences or tasks with a shared agreement of success that invigorates learners to develop these skills further (see Chapter 2). This means ensuring the relational conditions of collaborative learning are taught and developed (see Chapter 3), providing clear learning intentions and success criteria (see Chapter 4), and being intentional about the learning (see Chapter 5). Are you seeing how the pieces fit together? When we provide feedback to learners as they practice these prosocial skills, we further enhance positive interdependence and promotive interaction, and, ultimately, we boost achievement related to both the individual and collective learning (Johnson & Johnson, 2009).

Successful collaborative learning experiences are designed to include scaffolds to support these prosocial skills. John recognizes now that his algebra students might have thrived in a collaborative learning environment if he had taught prosocial skills and subskills, designed his collaborative tasks to include scaffolds to support these skills, and provided ongoing coaching in these skills. For example, as John's students were working on the mathematical modeling of an authentic scenario, he should have moved around the room and encouraged individual members to give their perspective, checked on the understanding of specific learners, and modeled these skills himself when groups seemed to need additional support. After completing a task, he should have led them in a debriefing of what they had learned, providing them an opportunity to do the following, as research recommends:

- Critically examine what went well during the task,
- Set individual and group goals for the next collaborative learning experience, and

- Provide feedback on the use of these skills during the day's learning and how they contributed to the team's progress toward the agreed-upon success criteria (Johnson, Johnson, & Holubec, 2013).

Let's look more at this reflective, feedback-based aspect of task processing.

Channels for Supportive Peer Communication

Even if learners are efficacious enough to seek help and have the necessary prosocial skills to support their peers, they need to be aware of the *channels* for providing such support. Simply put, they need to know how best to offer help. We have seen a couple of examples in our examples, when Zavian offered a response that provided a better approach to the problem and when Jackson's peers engaged in a conversation to share their perspectives on what a simile is and how they differentiate a simile from a metaphor.

Channels for supportive peer communication can be formal or informal:

- **Formal channels:** Learners provide support using a holistic or analytic rubric, and their comments are based on specific success criteria.
- **Informal channels:** Learners provide support through informal conversations about the experience or task.

Both formal and informal communication channels can be effective means of supportive peer feedback if students are explicitly taught the techniques to employ in various response channels like whole-group discussion, partner-talk, and written commentaries. What are supportive ways to ask questions, for example, or to offer suggestions? Figure 6.2 focuses on specific techniques that members of an SLC might use to respond to one another's writing, highlighting what the teacher should model and what the students need to understand. Teacher-led demonstrations of response techniques for small-group and partner settings can be helpful, as can monitoring students' responses in their groups and providing feedback, in the moment or in one-on-one conferences, to reinforce appropriate responses and redirect inappropriate ones. Over time, and with practice, students will learn to provide feedback to their peers. Of course, the question remains: how do teachers ensure the feedback students provide one another in their learning communities is effective?

FIGURE 6.2

Modeling Supportive Responses to a Peer's Written Work

Technique	What the teacher does	What students should understand
Evaluate the work/ respond to the work	Demonstrates that an evaluation focuses on the product and is driven by reference to rubric criteria, whereas a response focuses on the writer and is intended to be helpful	Evaluation is formal; response is informal, personable, and helps the writer improve.
Provide praise	Demonstrates how to talk about what you liked as a reader	General cheerleading is less helpful than pointing out specific positives.
Show you understand	Demonstrates how to talk about what you understood the piece to be about	Reflecting back the piece to the writer is helpful.
Ask questions	Demonstrates how to ask questions about parts or aspects of the writing you didn't understand	Focusing questions on the writer's purpose is helpful.
Provide suggestions	Demonstrates how to suggest a writer try specific techniques or make specific alterations	A good responder leaves the writer with ideas about what to do next.

Source: From "Responders Are Taught, Not Born," by J. Simmons, 2003, *Journal of Adolescent & Adult Literacy, 46*(8), p. 690. Copyright 2003 by International Reading Association/Wiley. Adapted with permission.

Qualities of Effective Feedback

Feedback provides information about a person's performance that can be used as a basis for improvement. Hattie (2012) explains the concept of *feedback* as information that should feed-forward learning, meaning it should equip the receiver to take action. What is interesting and important is that the giver of feedback does not have to be the teacher, nor does the sole receiver of feedback need to be a student. In SLCs, feedback can and should be exchanged among students as part of their collaboration in learning. There are several key points to keep in mind as you guide students' work in this area.

First, effective feedback is context-dependent, generated in response to an observable action, event, or process. The kind of feedback that promotes better collective learning emerges from well-designed tasks (see Chapter 2). In other words, teachers must ensure that the learning experience or task promotes student talk (academic discourse), includes the possibility of productive failure, elicits the right level of challenge, requires connections, sparks motivation, and promotes cooperation. Only then can peers draw out specific actions, events, or processes that allow them to amplify the learning of another member of the collective team.

Take, for example, an experience or task where learners sit around a table in a formation that resembles collective learning, but each is working independently and they simply "check" one another's responses for accuracy. There is no student action, event, or process for effective feedback. The task design denies students opportunities to provide support that would amplify the collective learning of the team.

Second, effective feedback conveys information that helps individual learners progress toward success criteria. Returning to Ms. Wenger's class, what if Christina had met Alexis's hesitant suggestion that they find the length of a rectangle's unknown sides by subtracting the length of a known side from the perimeter measurement by saying, "No, that's wrong; let me do it"? This "feedback" would not have contributed to Christina's specific understanding or the group's collective improvement. In addition, by retreating to an individual task, Christina would have closed her own learning off to future support from Zavian and Alexis.

Finally, effective feedback reinforces supportive relational conditions and promotes students' self-regulation. Thus, it should focus on elements of task execution, not the personal characteristics of the individual members of the group. In Christina's response ("They have different bottom numbers and that won't work, see?"), she focused on the task, not Alexis as a mathematics student or even her role within the group. Christina and Zavian pointed out that the *mathematical process needed correction,* not the person.

Susan Brookhart's (2017) exploration of feedback led her to three conclusions to keep in mind and convey to your learners:

- **Feedback should be timely.** In SLCs, make sure each member has opportunities to provide effective feedback to peers within the context of the learning experience or task. This peer-to-peer support must take place during the collective learning.
- **Feedback should be specific.** Comments offered by SLC members must be specific about the action, event, or process. They should focus on specific or additional steps that might improve the collaborative team's progress toward the shared agreement on the successful performance of a particular task.

- **Feedback should be constructive.** Again, feedback in an SLC focuses on the journey—actions, events, and processes—not individuals. By being constructive, peer-to-peer support serves a very useful purpose: moving the collective learning forward. If the goal in collaborative teams is the intentional collective learning that builds cognitive, metacognitive, and emotional regulation, constructive feedback ensures members progress in this learning. *Growth* implies that not all students may be where they need to be today, but they are farther along today than they were yesterday.

Types of Feedback

There are three types of feedback that are supportive of learning: task, process, and self-regulation. Which type of feedback to use depends upon where the collaborative learning team is in its progression toward the shared agreement on success: early in the progression versus later in the progression.

As collaborative teams initially engage in a learning experience, feedback should focus on the group's understanding of specific content, ideas, and terms. This **task feedback** is corrective and focuses on the accuracy of the group's work. The group relies on task feedback to solidify its conceptual understanding, which can come from analyzing examples and non-examples as well as discussion or dialogue about the procedural steps to solving a problem. This initial feedback provides clear information about the goals that provide guardrails or parameters for the team's next steps in the learning. Christina provided task feedback to Alexis by clearly articulating that the fractions could not be used in solving the problem as long as they had unlike denominators. Zavian, too, provided task feedback: "The bottom number is called the denominator, Christina. That's what we're supposed to call it."

Process feedback is critical to collaborative teams' ability to explore the why and the how of specific experiences and tasks. The group has likely identified clear boundaries between concepts and developed awareness of examples and non-examples associated with specific concepts. At this point, students have assimilated task feedback into their work to develop an initial understanding of content, terms, and ideas. In order to move beyond what is simply right or wrong, or what is an example or a non-example, learners must receive and incorporate feedback that focuses on the process or strategies associated with accomplishing a specific task. Once Ms. Wenger's learners had clearly established the concept of like versus unlike denominators, their support shifted to how to approach the problem.

As teams of learners begin to develop proficiency with specific content, ideas, and terms, peer-to-peer support should increasingly shift to process feedback—focusing on learners' thinking, not just the accuracy of their responses. Often, this type of feedback does not sort out what is right or wrong; instead, it propels groups into student talk (academic discourse), the possibility of productive failure, the right level of challenge, connections, enhanced motivation, and promoted cooperation. For example, Emelio asked his fellow group members what strategies they used in making the calculations for a number of math problems, and whether the strategy worked well or whether a different strategy might be more efficient. During a social studies lesson, Justine asked one of her team members, Andrew, if he used the best primary or secondary sources to generate the historical inferences included in his essay, and if the difference in the type of source might affect the accuracy of the inference. Rather than focusing on the correct answer regarding the relationship between an independent and dependent variable, Paul asked Brad, "What is your thinking for that problem? How did you get that?"

Self-regulation feedback refers to a collaborative team's ability to know what to do when approaching a new and different problem, when stuck, or when having to apply understanding in a new way—without initially reaching out to the teacher. Eventually, collective learners practice metacognition through self-verbalization, self-questioning, and self-reflection. They take personal ownership of their learning, which provides increased motivation and understanding. The ability to think about their own thinking promotes learners' self-awareness, and it enables them to problem-solve around the learning experience or task and to understand what they need to do to complete the task. Alexis incorporated the task and process feedback provided by her peers to self-regulate her own learning and leveraged that learning to initiate the problem-solving process. Getting collaborative teams to be timely, specific, and constructive with their task, process, and self-regulatory feedback, however, requires that teachers intentionally prepare them to do so.

Peer Support Within a Gradual Release of Responsibility Framework

Ms. Wenger's learners did not simply arrive on the first day of 3rd grade and immediately support one another with timely, specific, and constructive feedback. This was a skill they had to develop. Ms. Wenger explained her approach:

I had to explicitly teach them about feedback, modeled effective feedback using my examples, and had them give feedback with me while looking at a math problem, and then, after some time, they eventually supported each other—with me prompting them.

The gradual release of responsibility model (see Chapter 1) stipulates that Ms. Wenger move from assuming all of the responsibility for supporting students in their learning to a situation in which her learners assume the responsibility for supporting each other. This gradual release may occur over a day, a week, a month, or the first half of a year. With every new class, Ms. Wenger begins by modeling the desired outcome. ("I always did this in my face-to-face classroom. I just needed to remember to do it virtually now," she added.) Although she wants her students to know "what, how, and when to jump in and support their peers, they aren't ready for this in September." Over time, her learners assume more responsibility in supporting their peers in a way that amplifies learning. At this point, learners are no longer simply learning about how to engage their peers, nor are they apprentices in shared learning about feedback. Instead, they recognize what, how, and when to offer feedback during collective learning experiences. The ideal conditions to ensure deep collective learning occur when learners apply what they have learned through focused and guided instruction about how to create those conditions.

The majority of feedback students receive during a school day is not actually from teachers but from their peers, and the majority of that feedback is inaccurate. According to Graham Nuthall (2007), up to 80 percent of feedback comes from peers, and 80 percent of the time peer feedback is wrong or inaccurate. If teachers do not prepare students to support each other in ways that amplify learning, it's a sure bet that collective learning will devolve into independent work or a complete breakdown in the relational conditions of the collaborative team. To evaluate whether your learners are ready to move forward in providing peer-to-peer support, consider the following:

- Have you modeled goal setting and progress monitoring? Students can set goals and use the tools that are provided to monitor their progress once they understand how to do so.
- Do all students in each group have access to shared agreements on success? When agreements about success are shared, students are more likely to allocate their cognitive resources toward the work at hand.
- Will your students use tools to self-assess, and if so, do they know how to use them? Teaching about such tools often is necessary before asking

students to engage in peer feedback, so they understand where they are in relationship to the criteria.

- Have you provided students with sentence frames, sentence starters, or guiding questions to support their support of peers? Having something to say and knowing how to say it are two different things, so these supports are often necessary.
- Have you set aside specific times for students to provide support to their peers? While planning the use of instructional minutes, remember to include time for students to provide feedback.
- Have you provided students with multiple opportunities to practice engaging in supportive relational conditions? Once taught, students need to practice supporting their peers. They also need feedback from peers, and from their teacher, as they develop this skill.

To ensure that learning occurs, think about the learning experiences and the tasks you design and consider how students will collaboratively engage in this learning. From there, what type of feedback will be necessary to move learners closer to the shared agreements of success? One teacher cannot possibly provide all the feedback for all learners all of the time, nor are students waiting for you to do so. Rather, if you thoughtfully prepare your learners to provide timely, specific, and constructive peer-to-peer support, you can share the learning that takes place in these intentional collective learning experiences.

Kindergarten teacher Bethany Cornish told us she spends "a lot of time helping my students deliver this support, a lot of time teaching them how to relate to their peers about their learning." Effective feedback is timely, specific, and constructive, and its continued effectiveness in improving the learning of the collaborative team depends upon its delivery. In Ms. Cornish's classroom, "My students recognize when their peers need support. However, the way they go about providing that support can and does shut down learners. And then they are done for the day." So, to support her learners in providing peer-to-peer support through effective delivery, Ms. Cornish focuses on three guiding questions for feedback (Hattie & Timperley, 2007):

1. Where are we going?

2. How are we doing?

3. Where do we go next?

As her learners begin to write in a variety of forms, including narrative and descriptive forms, Ms. Cornish will often engage them in a task that requires them to describe a scene selected by the team. Once they are finished, SLCs exchange their work and try to guess what other groups are describing. In this enhanced version of "I Spy," once groups guess what is being described in their peers' piece of writing, they then provide feedback on the descriptive writing. "So they have to know how to deliver this information in a way that will be heard by their peers, " Ms. Cornish noted.

She explained that for this particular task, the "Where are we going?" question "refers to what it means to successfully construct a piece of descriptive writing. I have to make sure that we come to an agreement on success and that they have ways to keep that in focus." Ms. Cornish uses exemplars, anchor charts, and checklists, and her learners can choose the supports that best fit the needs of their group. The main goal is for her learners to deliver support that is specific to the success criteria. "They are kindergartners, so I have to make sure extraneous feedback that is not related to where we are going in our writing does not distract us from our work."

As Ms. Cornish's learners work on their descriptive writing, they offer peer support using the exemplars, anchor charts, or checklists to respond to the "How are we doing?" question.

Samantha: We don't use good descriptive words in our sentences. We should say the color and how big the tree is.

Ava: How do you spell *purple*?

Dylan: [Making the sound for *p*] I think it is *p-e-r.* . . . That's all I know. But don't forget the *p* goes below the line.

Samantha: Why purple? We want them to guess the tree outside, right?

Ava: Oh, yeah. It's green and brown. But I can only see part from here.

Dylan: Maybe we only describe what we can see now? Like, it is something bigger than a person.

Ava: And has different colors of green.

Samantha: It is in the ground.

Dylan: Yeah! In the ground but goes to the sky.

Ms. Cornish uses gradual release of responsibility to help her students build the language necessary to deliver feedback to further her group's focus on progress toward the success criteria. She explained her approach:

I begin with a think-aloud and directly teach the language associated with this type of exchange. This can be as simple as using this language during morning meeting and as complex as using student exemplars and pointing out where learners have met the success criteria.

From there, Ms. Cornish provides her learners with scaffolded support that gradually releases them to engage in this dialogue with their peers: sentence frames, sentence starters, guiding questions, and then independent dialogue.

The third question ("Where do we go next?") is also dependent on the shared agreement of success. Ms. Cornish explained that her learners quickly point out what needs to be adjusted in their work "because they have a clear understanding of what success looks like. I find that if I devote time to goal setting and progress monitoring, they are able to quickly pick up this part of the process," she said. Figure 6.3 provides some examples of different learners providing peer-to-peer support across different settings, using the three guiding questions.

Moving Forward ...

To design a learning environment where peers are supporting peers requires that teachers first create a situation where learners recognize the positive interdependence of the SLC: the idea that every member of the team is needed to meet the day's success criteria. We can foster this interdependence by ensuring that there are measures in place that hold both individual team members and the collective team accountable. In turn, this encourages promotive interaction, the willingness of the team to facilitate one another's contributions through peer-to-peer support. In the end, learners are more likely to seek help, apply prosocial skills as they use available and appropriate channels for offering support, and deliver effective feedback.

Feedback on and for learning is crucial to sustaining learning. Peer-to-peer support during collective learning experiences is crucial to sustaining collaborative learning, and it is built on the following:

- Experiences and tasks that invigorate learning;
- Supportive relational conditions that advance academic and social-emotional learning;
- Shared agreements of success in groups;
- Intentional collective learning that builds cognitive, metacognitive, and emotional regulation; and

FIGURE 6.3

Effective Peer-to-Peer Feedback: How to Answer Guiding Questions

Scenario	Where are we going?	How are we doing?	Where do we go next?
The supporting details in the group's argument do not align with their position statement for a debate about deforestation.	Remember, we have examples of high-quality presentations that we can use as models for our own work.	Our position statement does not align with the supporting details.	Let's look at the examples and exemplars. What do we notice that is different from or similar to our position statement and our supporting details? How do these presentations align their supporting details? What do we need to change?
During a chemistry laboratory investigation, the group has a large percent error in their calculation of density.	We are calculating the density of an unknown substance using the relationship between mass and volume.	Our numbers are way off. Did we zero out the scale between trials?	Let's check our numbers and redo our measurements. This time, there should be two of us making these measurements—we can check each other. The relationship should be linear.
The group can identify only one factor that led to the fall of the Soviet Union.	The teacher told us yesterday that the fall of a country is the result of many different and related events or influences.	There are several contributing factors leading to the fall of the Soviet Union. There has to be more than one—we have missed something.	What resources could we use to identify additional factors leading to the fall of the Soviet Union? We should divide and conquer to make sure we don't miss something.

- Leadership skills all students need to succeed, alone and together (we'll get to this in the next chapter).

Supporting all learners invokes the principle of gradual release of responsibility. As learners develop more learning strategies and metacognitive strategies, they will need less support. In the end, peer-to-peer support will rest predominantly in the hands of students as they become self-regulated learners, developing and executing their group's plan through the learning progression and beyond. As teachers, we can empower our learners to engage in this peer-to-peer support by designing collective learning experiences with criteria that help them clearly see where they are going, how they are doing, and where to go next.

The following questions are a good place to start, and you can use them going forward to monitor interactions in your face-to-face or virtual classroom and inform your decisions relative to the peer supports necessary for student learning communities to thrive.

1. Do your students seek help from one another? What types of help?

2. Which prosocial skills do your students possess and which do you need to teach?

3. What interaction patterns do you see in the groups? What communication skills need development?

4. What types of feedback do your students provide one another? What might you do to increase the quality of the feedback peers provide one another?

Leadership Skills
for SLC Success

The final piece necessary for student learning communities (SLCs) to be successful is for individual members to be prepared to step up and step into leadership roles.

Think about the successful collaborative and collective learning experiences of the teachers and classrooms we have shared in the preceding chapters: to support the SLC, individual students leveraged not only their content knowledge, skills, and understandings but their leadership skills as well. In each instance, an individual student activated the work of the group by leading the rest of the team to engage in **critical thinking, creative thinking, communication,** and—most important—**collaboration.** These four skills, plus **citizenship,** have been identified by Battelle for Kids (2020) as the "5 Cs" that describe the portrait of a graduate best prepared to engage and succeed in a today's world. These traits are also the leadership skills learners need to succeed alone and as part of an SLC. (In our work, we use the phrase *civic engagement* rather than citizenship to ensure that students understand that we are not talking about being a citizen of a specific country.)

We have a new appreciation of the "5 Cs" as essential traits of leaders in the virtual environments in our own professional work. How crucial will these be for our own students? "Future proofing" is a concept used in many industries to describe efforts to mitigate the effects of possible future negative events by equipping systems with features that won't make them obsolete. In education, future-proofing efforts have been largely devoted to technology systems.

In the spring of 2020, when in-person schooling everywhere was shut down in response to the novel coronavirus pandemic, the benefits of future proofing could be seen in districts that were able to connect virtually with their students and shift learning to an online mode. It is nothing short of remarkable that so many districts were able to act as quickly as they did. And while by no means have we experienced 100-percent coverage, especially for vulnerable students, it should be stressed that the investment educational systems have made in technology made it plausible. It would have been impossible to have managed it at all 10 years ago.

But it has become increasingly clear that educators need to think carefully about how we future-proof our students, not just our hardware. The co-related abilities of being able to collaborate productively with others and to lead one's own learning have become the tipping point for schooling. In considering the inequities that intermittent or full-time distance learning can amplify, it is crucial that we be intentional about equipping all learners, and especially those who are underserved, with the cognitive and metacognitive tools they need to be successful in extraordinary circumstances *and* when schooling follows familiar rhythms and is conducted in brick-and-mortar classrooms. To ensure deep collective learning, our students need opportunities to develop and use the 5 Cs—critical thinking, creative thinking, communication, collaboration, and citizenship (or civic engagement, our preferred term)—in all learning environments.

Julia Urban and her instructional coach, Justine Juart, decided to use SLCs to support their high school students' individual and collective learning about living systems, specifically the classification of living things. These two teachers set the stage by providing their learners with a scenario:

> Ms. Urban and Ms. Juart do not have any ideas about how to teach the classification of living things. How do we help each other understand the reason living things are classified into five kingdoms and how this helps us as scientists?

This activity is designed so that students must assume the role of "teacher" and work in their SLCs to design and implement the best way to teach others this content. The SLCs will have to create "check-in" assessments, journal notes, and ways to review important content—just to name a few of the specific expectations.

When learners have the opportunity to take on the role of the teacher, it almost always invigorates learning. However, to ensure that each collaborative team knows where to direct their energy, Ms. Urban and Ms. Juart first establish a shared agreement on success (see Figure 7.1).

FIGURE 7.1

Shared Agreement for Success: Classifying Living Things

WHAT DO WE NEED TO DO?

1. **ANALYZE** the *Content Standards* to understand what we need to learn during this unit.

2. **RESEARCH** and learn about **YOUR KINGDOM** using videos, online sources, books, and more so that you feel confident in the information you have to teach your "students."

3. Work in your **TEAM** to **COMPLETE** the *Research Page* with all of the important information about your kingdom.

4. **PLAN YOUR LESSON!** How will you present information to your "students"? What gestures will you use for important *vocabulary?* What do you want your "students" to include in their notebooks? Who is responsible for which *tasks* on your team?

5. **TEACH YOUR LESSON**. Present all of the important information to your "students" in a creative and engaging way.

6. **CREATE A REVIEW TASK** that helps reinforce the most important ideas from your *Research Page* and teaching.

7. **REVIEW** with your "students" by presenting and guiding them through the **REVIEW TASK**.

8. **ASSESS** your "students." Create seven assessment questions from the most important ideas from your research, teaching, and review.
   *Double-check your *Content Standard* bullets: are you hitting the most important content, skills, and understandings?

9. **REFLECT** on how well your "students" understand what you taught them. How did they perform as "students"? How successful were **YOU** as a teacher?

10. **CELEBRATE** how much you and your "students" learned throughout this adventure!!

This task requires that collaborative teams engage in critical thinking about the learning expectations related to classification of living things and the five kingdoms, the research process necessary to enhance their own learning, and the means by which they will assess the learning of themselves and their peers ("students"). It demands creative thinking in the design and development of a learning experience that helps their peers acquire content, skills, and understandings. Communication among the group members and with other groups is paramount for the successful completion of this task.

Notably, this lesson could be used in either a face-to-face classroom or a virtual one. Take a step back and look at this task through the lens of leadership. How is it designed to activate the leadership skills in learners that they will need to be successful alone and together?

As you might suspect, this learning experience, which requires students to take the reins of their own learning and successfully operate in an SLC, wasn't one that Ms. Urban and Ms. Juart executed at the start of the school year. They waited until after they had intentionally fostered, nurtured, and developed their students' leadership skills. And before you write this task off as too complex or difficult to implement in your own classroom, consider how you might help your students develop the skills they would need to complete it successfully. Leaders activate others. Not only can you teach your students to activate the specific behaviors and actions such a lesson requires, you can teach them to activate these same behaviors and actions among their peers to ensure everyone's success.

Activating Critical Thinking

Engaging in critical thinking, whether independently or collectively, requires students to apply the skills of analyzing, interpreting, inferring, explaining, self-regulating, and problem solving. Ms. Urban focuses on critical thinking from the beginning of the school year. She explained:

> On the very first day of school, I provide and model sentence stems, sentence starters, and guiding questions for every topic we learn. In science, I ask them to analyze phenomena. In mathematics, I ask them to interpret their answers. In language arts, I ask them to make inferences and cite evidence from the text. In social studies, I ask them to explain their thinking when discussing historical events.

As the school's instructional coach, Ms. Juart supports teachers as they deliberately work to develop critical thinking in their learners. Her focus is to "break down critical thinking into necessary subskills. This helps teachers to provide intentional and manageable opportunities for learners to get to this type of thinking." For example, she has developed a progression for breaking down inferring into subskills (see Figure 7.2) to support teachers in scaffolding learning for the process: from teacher-led to teacher-guided to student-led.

FIGURE 7.2

A Progression for Inferring

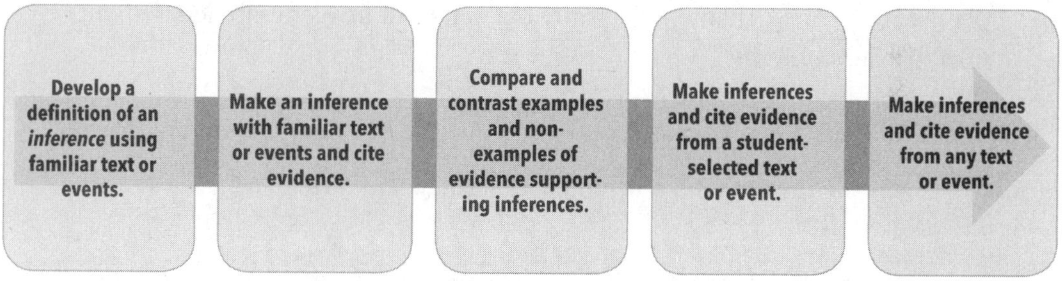

Develop a definition of an *inference* using familiar text or events.

Make an inference with familiar text or events and cite evidence.

Compare and contrast examples and non-examples of evidence supporting inferences.

Make inferences and cite evidence from a student-selected text or event.

Make inferences and cite evidence from any text or event.

At the beginning of the school year, Ms. Urban works with Ms. Juart in planning lessons to develop her learners' skills in making inferences and citing evidence. "By the time we get to the collaborative task on the five kingdoms, this skill comes natural to them," she pointed out. In addition, the teachers engage their learners in questions that both model critical thinking and inject a healthy level of intellectual skepticism in the learning community—questions like these:

- Where did this information come from? Is this a reputable source?
- Is the author trying to persuade you? If so, is the argument reliable?
- What evidence supports the thinking? Is there evidence that does not support the thinking?
- What other ways can we think about this problem?

This modeling allows Ms. Urban and Ms. Juart's learners to begin integrating critical thinking into their academic discourse, while at the same time ensuring that the discourse focuses on the experience, tasks, or thinking and not the person (i.e., effective peer-to-peer support).

Activating Creative Thinking

Creativity has two main components: the development of a new idea not directly generated from something or someone else and the establishment that the idea is of value or use (Plucker, Beghetto, & Dow, 2004). For learners, this requires acquiring considerable knowledge, skills, and understandings and then viewing current experiences and tasks in a flexible manner that allows them to bring this knowledge to the current work of the learning community. To design and develop learning experiences that help their "students" acquire the content, skills, and understandings, the learners in Ms. Urban and Ms. Juart's classroom need to pull together considerable knowledge about the content associated with the five kingdoms as well as knowledge about how people learn. Ms. Urban enjoys watching her students generate ideas about how to teach content:

> Some create their own approach, while others use something they have seen me do. I often wonder if those who come up with new approaches simply did not find mine helpful. Or did they have ideas for new ways of learning?

So how do teachers foster creativity? There are many small techniques and strategies we can employ in the classroom that, when taken together, create a learning environment that encourages creativity. Just as Ms. Urban and Ms. Juart scaffold their learners' progress toward critical thinking, they also employ specific strategies to promote it:

- **Mistakes are not only welcomed but treated as opportunities.** When a student makes a mistake, learners try and come up with a question, problem, or scenario where that mistake would be the "better" or "correct" answer.
- **There is a parking lot for learners' questions.** Throughout the day, when learners finish a task early or find a question in the parking lot that relates to what they are working on, they are encouraged to answer that question and be prepared to share with the class.
- **Brainstorming is an essential element.** Ms. Urban and Ms. Juart frequently ask open-ended questions that require learners to brainstorm, combine ideas, and modify their thinking.
- **Learning is a process.** These learners see that learning is a process because they receive effective feedback and are allowed to revise their work.

Ms. Juart described these strategies as "ways to let our students know that it is OK to think outside the box."

Activating Communication

Ms. Urban and Ms. Juart's students need to communicate both effectively and efficiently in order to work together and complete all the parts of the task.

At the heart of SLCs is the communication among individual community members. Every teacher knows that getting learners to communicate about their learning beyond requests or demands for supplies can be a challenge. It is important to note that there is a difference in supporting learners as they engage in academic discourse and building students' leadership skills to be able to communicate around a common task. Communicating requires that SLC members build background knowledge and explore different perspectives on a topic. In addition, they must engage in verbal communication that is purposeful, clear, and concise. Then, as they engage in academic discourse, they must practice the skill of active listening to ensure everyone understands the different perspectives of the team. Asking clarifying, summarizing, probing, or elaborating questions provides additional opportunities for active listeners to advance their understanding, and, at the same time, helps individuals fine-tune their own thinking. Finally, SLCs must be able to use multiple means of communicating their ideas and their thinking (e.g., written communication, other digital tools).

Ms. Urban and Ms. Juart use the gradual release of responsibility framework (Fisher & Frey, 2014) to develop their learners' communication skills (see Figure 7.3). Ms. Urban noted:

> In the early part of the year, we provide learners with sentence stems for summarizing, elaborating, or clarifying their thinking. Then, Ms. Juart provides a question cube where each face of the cube contains a mix of clarifying, summarizing, probing, and elaborating questions.

These supports, paired with an anchor chart that provides cues for active listening, initiate the development of the skills learners need to explore and communicate different perspectives in a purposeful, clear, and concise manner.

FIGURE 7.3

A Progression for Activating Communication Skills in SLCs

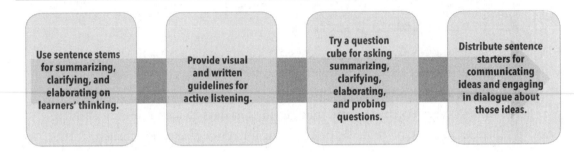

Activating Collaboration

It is one thing to develop the skills of critical thinking, creative thinking, and communication with among members of an SLC and other learning communities. Supporting learners in understanding what it truly means to collaborate, however, is a bit different. Collaboration among learners suffers when learners have different goals, as when some learners seek to develop mastery in the content while others just want to complete the task or socialize (see Levy, Kaplan, & Patrick, 2000). When learners have different goals, they are less likely to lend peer-to-peer support and more likely to simply sit in a group configuration while working independently on their part of the task.

Thomas Alexander, a high school mathematics teacher, acknowledged that "some groups simply work on a problem independently. They don't even recognize that all four students in the group have submitted a different answer." Brian Patterson, a high school chemistry teacher, noted a similar challenge in his groups: "The student who 'gets it' dominates the conversation and does all of the work. There is no collaboration."

Because many learners simply do not have the skills necessary to effectively collaborate at first, teachers need to support this development by implementing cooperative learning structures that progress from simple to complex, from teacher-directed to student-led. Starting with "shoulder partners" or a think–pair–share activity sets the stage for exposing students to what it means to work together with a peer and focus on a common cause. From there, engaging learners in reciprocal teaching or using a jigsaw strategy enhances the complexity of their collaboration, allowing for more responsibility to fall on individual students for the ways in which they engage with their peers. Ultimately, these intentionally selected learning structures help to develop collaboration skills in learners. Let's look at specific examples.

Think–Pair–Share

As an instructional coach, Ms. Juart has a lot of interactions with teachers and different configurations of students. She has noticed that "when students get comfortable exchanging ideas with their peer partner, they become more comfortable talking together about a guiding question or problem."

Ms. Urban often has her learners begin by reviewing their notes, thumbing through a reading passage associated with the content, reviewing a worked example, or looking over a visual or diagram—this is the "think" part. After a minute or two, she asks her learners to summarize the information contained in the notes, reading passage, worked example, or visual with their peer partner. She explained, "Using a question that they have to answer—first individually and then together—helps learners to focus on working together in this brief amount of time, gives them opportunities to take ownership over their learning, and allows them to feel more confident when sharing. The students are also building relationships while talking about their ideas."

The next step is to ask students to identify and highlight critical points together; this is the "pair and share." As they become more comfortable with this routine, the quality of their responses, conversations, and peer-to-peer support will increase.

Reciprocal Teaching

As learners effectively collaborate with a peer partner, teachers can begin to enhance the complexity of the collaboration through reciprocal teaching.

Mr. Patterson, the chemistry teacher, implemented reciprocal teaching to support his goal of having all learners engaging in a conversation rather than allowing a single individual to dominate the work. As he explained, "To provide context for oxidation-reduction reactions, I provide groups of learners with a science-based text that discusses the impact of oxidation-reduction reactions on everyday life." His approach is to divide the text into different sections and ask each group to pause at the end of their assigned section and discuss its content using the following strategies:

- Summarize the particular section of text, highlighting what the segment was about and what you've learned from this segment as it relates to oxidation-reduction reactions.

- Pose questions at the literal, structural, or inferential levels about the section of text, emphasizing what things the section makes you wonder about.
- Identify information and ideas that need clarification. Which ideas did not make sense? What parts of the text did you find confusing?
- Predict the content of the next segment of the text and what possible new learning will come from the text.

For Ms. Urban and Ms. Juart, reciprocal teaching provides an opportunity for their learners to activate critical thinking skills at the same time they are activating collaboration skills. To help learners who need a lot of structure, the teachers provide graphic organizers and guiding questions. Ms. Urban noted that "over time, they no longer need those tools. This tells us they are ready for more student-led collaboration. That is when we introduce the jigsaw."

Jigsaw

The jigsaw strategy is another learning routine that relies on an expert group and a base group. The steps in the process are as follows:

1. Divide the learning into four or five parts. This will be the number of expert groups needed for the jigsaw.

2. Assign learners to a base group of three, four, or five students.

3. Assign learners within each base group to "expert" groups and inform each group what expertise they will need to develop (e.g., in a chemistry class, a type of reaction). Each member of the base group is assigned to one of the expert groups.

4. After learners review their expert material individually, have the expert groups meet and collaborate to complete a task related to their area of expertise (e.g., figure out how to teach the base group about the specific type of reaction).

5. Embed measures of accountability to ensure that hesitant learners become actively engaged in the learning.

6. Provide group support for material that may be difficult to master alone and help students master content in greater depth.

7. Provide time for expert groups to complete the activity and prepare their teaching strategy.

8. Have experts return to their base group and present their new learning.

9. Have expert groups meet again to debrief the experience and reflect on how their area of expertise fit into the larger picture of the learning experience.

Mr. Alexander, the high school mathematics teacher, also uses the jigsaw strategy to support his learners, assigning them to expert groups for particular mathematical functions (e.g., logarithmic, rational, exponential, polynomial). "Each learner understands that he or she will be responsible to share the knowledge they have gained with the base group," Mr. Alexander said.

It is important to note that the last part of the jigsaw—the debrief or return to the expert group to engage in critical thinking about how their particular expertise fit into the bigger picture of the learning—is often overlooked. Ms. Urban and Ms. Juart stress that this reflective step is essential and a precursor to successful SLCs.

Think–pair–share, reciprocal teaching, and jigsaw are only three examples of learning routines that provide a framework for learners to effectively collaborate with their peers. One common characteristic of such structures is that it provides a meaningful way for students to actively engage with one another—building the "muscles" they need for successful collaboration. As students develop these skills and become more efficient at using them on a daily basis, the need to provide such structures will fade. Individuals will step forward to suggest and lead these kinds of exchanges on their own. In this way, these arrangements serve as springboard for student-led teams, equipping them with habits and skills they can use to develop and execute their own student-driven projects, or what are often referred to as passion/purpose projects.

Activating Civic Engagement

Civic engagement speaks to the overall investment in the work of the SLC. SLCs aim for members to be invested in the task such that they feel intrinsically motivated and personally accountable for ensuring that the learning community meets the agreed-upon learning objective and success criteria.

Ms. Urban noted that when she's assigned the classification and five kingdoms task, "The learners each recognize that they have a responsibility for doing their part and moving the work of the group forward. They are also aware that their efforts will impact the success of their peers as they take on the role of the teacher. You can hear this in their conversations and observe this in their actions." Here's a part of one such conversation. See how many key features of civic engagement you notice.

Stefan: Sarah, is this the information you're looking for? Does this work for you?

Sarah: Yes, that is really good, but we have to make it interesting so that we capture people's attention.

Stefan: Oh yeah, good point. I'm on it. I'm sure I can find weird animals that aren't easy to classify because they don't look like animals. Can I have a few extra minutes to look harder?

Sarah: Sure, but remember we have to be ready to give each other feedback in the group by 10:45.

Stefan: Yep, Michaela is watching the time, and Sheerie says she will have the check-in questions done soon.

In this very short exchange, which Ms. Urban and Ms. Juart pointed out is representative of how their learners interact with one another all the time, here are the examples of civic engagement we see:

- Sarah, Stefan, Michaela, and Sheerie showed support for the norms of the SLC: timelines, deadlines, division of labor, and peer-to-peer support. Sarah defended those norms by reminding Stefan that they were approaching a deadline, which Michaela was monitoring.
- The SLC members strived to stay informed by checking in on each other and, in Stefan's case, ensuring that his efforts were aligned with the agreed-upon learning objective and their collective work toward the success criteria.
- Each member of the SLC was actively participating. This could go without saying, but it shouldn't. Civic engagement requires you to show up.
- Stefan and Sarah demonstrated respect for each other; it's clear they see each other as valuable members of the SLC.

Civic engagement, similarly, is vital in Mr. Patterson's chemistry classroom. The class currently meets one day a week in a face-to-face environment to complete labs. He explained that when he places students in SLCs to address an open-ended problem or track their progress within a particular unit, "they must support and defend the norms of the group to ensure that as they work in the laboratory they are exercising the utmost care with chemicals and glassware." He pointed out that in order to perform complex mathematical calculations in chemistry, his learners need to stay informed and show respect for each other, as some of their classmates need more peer-to-peer support in grasping concepts.

Mr. Alexander also commented on the importance of mutual respect, noting that "in mathematics, they have to invest in the success of the whole group and be willing to participate by offering peer support and then participate by speaking up when they are struggling with a concept."

Assigning, Developing, and Assuming Roles in SLCs

Ms. Urban, Ms. Juart, Mr. Patterson, and Mr. Alexander share a common approach for activating civic engagement within their SLCs. They start by assigning roles to each member of every SLC. Our own experiences testify to the wisdom of this approach. As learners assume the responsibility of dividing the labor of the SLC, taking on individual responsibilities, and stepping up or into leadership roles, they must engage in deliberate practice in this process. Therefore, it's best to be purposeful in group composition (see Chapter 6) and take the following factors into consideration:

- What specific skills are needed to engage in this experience or task (e.g., creativity, critical thinking)?
- What are the growth opportunities for the members of the SLC? In other words, is this an opportunity for developing specific skills in certain learners?
- Does everyone in the class understand each role and its deliverables? Is it necessary to have a whole-group discussion on what it means, for example, to be a "discussion leader"?
- What supports are available to learners as they develop their skills within their specific role? How will the work of the SLC be monitored, and how will learners obtain support in their roles?

Figure 7.4 provides the SLC roles, tasks, and deliverables that Ms. Urban and Ms. Juart have developed for their class. Of course, the specific roles you might use for a specific experience or task will depend on the nature of the content, the shared agreement of success, and the particular skills you are trying to develop and activate in your learners.

FIGURE 7.4

SLC Roles, Tasks, and Deliverables

Role	Tasks and deliverables
Discussion director or leader	• Directs, leads, or guides the activities of the SLC. • Decides on the division of labor for the day's work. • Develops a set of critical thinking questions (not yes, no, or one-word response questions) that encourage group members to maintain the norms of the group, move forward in their individual work, and stay informed about the collective work of the SLC.
Big-idea builder	• Develops a list of the big ideas or the "must-know" content. • Creates a visual or written summary of the content. • Prepares a response to the question "Why is this material important?" This should represent the application of the content to things outside the experience or task.
Word wizard	• Identifies key vocabulary, terms, or concepts. • Prepares a description of each vocabulary, term, or concept. • Creates a visual for each item. • Identifies a specific example of each item. • Provides further information as needed about each vocabulary item, term, or concept.
Visualizer	• Creates a concept map of the learning by showing how different concepts and ideas link together. • Interacts with different group members to ask clarifying, elaborating, or probing questions. • Verbalizes how certain concepts are connected together on the concept map.
Highlighter	• Identifies important readings and resources and marks them with sticky notes or tabs. • Summarizes the research for the SLC. • Provides a justification of why particular readings, sections, or passages were selected.

We want to stress that these roles are a means to develop skills as much as they are to execute tasks. Learners need time to step into these roles, practice them, and grow into greater proficiency. Mr. Alexander uses the assignment of roles to activate creativity in mathematics:

I often assign the role of making connections to learners who do not see the application of mathematics beyond the worksheet, textbook problem set, or test. I want them to explore how exponential functions help explain phenomena in the world. What I often see, over time, is that this role motivates learners to naturally ask how this applies to the real world without me even bringing it up.

Sustaining Student Learning Communities

A final topic we want to tackle before wrapping up this book is the sustainability of collective learning. As teachers strive to ensure that deep collective learning is due to design and not just chance, how do they sustain this collaborative learning beyond a specific task, unit, school year, or the walls of the classroom? The answer lies in very important practices that learners engage in—not just on a given day or in a specific physical or virtual classroom but as part of every learning experience. These are practices we want to become part of how we "do learning" in our schools and classrooms (see Figure 7.5).

FIGURE 7.5

What Student Learning Communities Need and Can Achieve

Conditions for a successful SLC	The teacher's role	The eventual outcome
Experiences and tasks that encourage student dialogue	Plan, design, and implement experiences and tasks that invigorate learning.	Learners will seek their own authentic experiences that promote deep learning related to the learning outcomes.
Supportive relational conditions that empower learning	Foster relational conditions that advance academic, social, and emotional learning in the classroom every day.	Learners will imitate and utilize relational behaviors with their peers.
Shared agreements about success	Provide explicit instruction on goal setting and opportunities to practice progress monitoring.	Learners will set their own goals and monitor the learning progress of their collaborative group, making adjustments when needed.
Intentional collective learning that builds cognitive and metacognitive skills	Ensure that learning experiences and tasks require collaboration and include opportunities for individuals to leverage their strengths.	Learners will know when to use which of their individual strengths to engage successfully in the experience or task.
Intentional leveraging of peer supports that amplify learning	Give and receive feedback aligned to the specific needs both individual and groups of learners.	Learners will give and receive peer feedback that moves the group closer to reaching its goals.
The activation of leadership skills students need to succeed—alone and together	Identify and develop specific leadership skills and strategies that students need to succeed.	Learners will apply those skills at the right time and in a way that leads to the success of the group.

The ability of students to engage in sustained collaborative learning that, in the end, is completely driven by the team and not by the teacher requires practices that promote in students the kind of thinking that looks inward as well as outward and asks them to draw from the collective wisdom of their peers to accelerate and expand their learning.

Moving Forward . . .

If the ultimate goal is for individual members of the SLC to step up and step into leadership roles, teachers must do as they have always done and provide opportunities for learners to tap into their strengths, identify areas of growth, and deliberately engage in experiences or tasks that capitalize on strengths and foster growth. As we have said throughout this book, SLCs attend not only to academic learning but social and emotional learning as well. When working to activate leadership skills for success as individuals and as a community, we teachers must scaffold this process to help every student build on the 5 Cs: critical thinking, creativity, communication, collaboration, and civic engagement. We cannot assume they will come to us with these skills at the ready. Development of these skills is part of the learning we pursue with our students as a step forward in future-proofing them.

The experiences of Ms. Urban, Ms. Juart, Mr. Patterson, and Mr. Alexander highlight that this process involves developing specific roles and deliverables that target the development of necessary leadership skills. As learners embrace these roles and successfully fulfill these roles, their self-efficacy around critical thinking or creativity, for example, goes up. Then, in the not-so-distant future, they begin to step up and step into these roles as a natural part of the SLC work. This cycle continues and creates the greatest probability that, when leadership is needed, members of the SLC will have the skills to lead and the ability to recognize when and where to use those skills.

The following questions are a good place to start your leadership activation work. You can use them going forward to monitor interactions in your face-to-face or virtual classroom and inform your decisions relative to the leadership skills and opportunities necessary for student learning communities to thrive.

1. How much critical thinking do your students do in their learning communities? How do you know? How will you support them and increase their ability to think critically?

2. How much creative thinking do your students do in their learning communities? How do you know? How will you support them and increase their ability to think creatively?

3. How well do your students communicate in their learning communities? How do you know? How will you support them and increase their ability to communicate effectively?

4. How much collaboration do your students exhibit in their learning communities? How do you know? How will you support them and increase their ability to collaborate with others?

5. How much civic engagement do your students display in their learning communities? How do you know? How will you support them and increase their ability to engage civically?

6. How will you sustain student learning communities over time such that this becomes a natural feature of the ways in which students learn?

We have come to the end of this book, but not the end of the journey. Much like the ongoing work of professional learning communities for adults, student learning communities are always a work in progress. All of us can always improve the interactions we have with others, further the thinking of our peers, and keep enhancing and expanding our collective understanding.

That is the power of collective wisdom.

That is why student learning communities matter!

References

Adams-Byers, J., Whitsell, S. S., & Moon, S. M. (2004). Gifted students' perceptions of the academic and social/emotional effects of homogeneous and heterogeneous grouping. *Gifted Child Quarterly, 48*(1), 7–20. doi:10.1177/001698620404800102

Arterberry, M., Cain, K., & Chopko, S. (2007). Collaborative problem solving in five-year-old children: Evidence of social facilitation and social loafing. *Educational Psychology, 27*(5), 577–596. doi:10.1080/01443410701308755

Battelle for Kids. (2020, March). *Portrait of a graduate.* Retrieved from https://portraitofagraduate.org/

Bennett, N., & Cass, A. (1989). The effects of group composition on group interactive processes and pupil understanding. *British Educational Research Journal, 15*(1), 19–32. doi:10.1080/0141192890150102

Billing, D. (2007). Teaching for transfer of core/key skills in higher education: Cognitive skills. *Higher Education, 53,* 483–516. doi:10.1007/s10734-005-5628-5

Boekaerts, M. (2002). The on-line motivation questionnaire: A self-report instrument to assess students' context sensitivity. In P. R. Pintrich & M. L. Maehr (Eds.), *Advances in motivation and achievement: Vol. 12. New directions in measures and methods* (pp. 77–120). Stamford, CT: JAI Press.

Boud, D., Keogh, R., & Walker, D. (Eds.). (2013). *Reflection: Turning experience into learning.* New York: Routledge.

Bransford, J. D., Brown, A. L., & Cocking, R. R. (2000). *How people learn: Brain, mind, experience, and school.* Washington, DC: National Academy Press.

Brookhart, S. (2017). *How to give effective feedback to your students* (2nd ed.). Alexandria, VA: ASCD.

Clarke, S. (2014). *Outstanding formative assessment: Culture and practice.* London: Hodder.

Claxton, G. (2017). *The learning power approach: Teaching learners to teach themselves.* Thousand Oaks, CA: Corwin.

Coates, G. (2005). Adventures in communication. *Connect, 19*(1), 11–13.

Cohen, E. G., & Lotan, R. A. (2014). *Designing groupwork. Strategies for the heterogeneous classroom* (3rd ed.). New York: Teachers College Press.

Corwin Visible Learning. (2019, June). *250+ influences on student achievement.* Retrieved from https://us.corwin.com/sites/default/files/250_influences_chart_june_2019.pdf

Curtis, C. P. (1999). *Bud, not Buddy.* New York: Delacorte Books.

Davis, B. G. (1993). *Tools for teaching.* San Francisco: Jossey-Bass.

Daywalt, D. (2013). *The day the crayons quit.* New York: Philomel.

Dore, R. A., Amendum, S. J., Golinkoff, R. M., & Hirsh-Pasek, K. (2018). Theory of mind: A hidden factor in reading comprehension? *Educational Psychology Review, 30,* 1067–1089. doi:10.1007/s10648-018-9443-9

Durlak, J. A., Weissberg, R. P., Dymnicki, A. B., Taylor, R. D., & Schellinger, K. B. (2011). The impact of enhancing students' social and emotional learning: A meta-analysis of school-based universal interventions. *Child Development, 82*(1), 405–432.

EL Education. (n.d.). *Collaborative culture: Norms.* Retrieved from https://eleducation .org/resources/collaborative-culture-norms#

Elbaum, B. E., Schumm, J. S., & Vaughn, S. (1997). Urban middle-elementary students' perceptions of grouping formats for reading instruction. *Elementary School Journal, 97*(5), 475–500. doi:10.1086/461877

Fay, N., Garrod, S., & Carletta, J. (2000). Group discussion as interactive dialogue or as serial monologue: The influence of group size. *Psychological Science, 11*(6), 481–486. doi:10.1111/1467-9280.00292

Fisher, D., & Frey, N. (2014). *Better learning through structured teaching: A framework for the gradual release of responsibility* (2nd ed.). Alexandria, VA: ASCD.

Fisher, D. B., Frey, N., & Everlove, S. (2009). *Productive group work: How to engage students, build teamwork, and promote understanding.* Alexandria, VA: ASCD.

Fisher, D., Frey, N., & Hattie, J. (2016). *Visible learning for literacy: Implementing the practices that work best to accelerate student learning.* Thousand Oaks, CA: Corwin.

Fisher, D., Frey, N., & Rothenberg, C. (2008). *Content-area conversations: Discussion-based lessons for diverse language learners.* Alexandria, VA: ASCD.

Flavell, J. H. (1979). Metacognition and cognitive monitoring. A new area of cognitive-developmental inquiry. *American Psychologist, 34*(10), 906–911. doi:10.1037/0003-066X.34.10.906

Flood, J., Lapp, D., Flood, S., & Nagel, G. (1992). Am I allowed to group? Using flexible patterns for effective instruction. *The Reading Teacher, 45*(8), 608–616.

Frey, N., Fisher, D., & Nelson, J. (2013, March). It's all about the talk. *Kappan, 94*(6), 8–13.

Garrett, R., & Hong, G. (2016). Impacts of grouping and time on the math learning of language minority kindergartners. *Educational Evaluation and Policy Analysis, 38*(2), 222–244. doi:10.3102/0162373715611484

Gillies, R., & Ashman, A. (1996). Teaching collaborative skills to primary school children in classroom-based work groups. *Learning and Instruction, 6*(3), 187–200. doi:10.1016/0959-4752(96)00002-3

Gillies, R., & Ashman, A. (1998). Behavior and interactions of children in cooperative groups in lower and middle elementary grades. *Journal of Educational Psychology, 90*(4), 746–757. doi:10.1037/0022-0663.90.4.746

Gorney, C. (2008, August 3). The urge to merge. *New York Times.* Retrieved from https://www.nytimes.com/2008/08/03/magazine/03traffic-t.html

Government of South Australia, Office for Education, Department for Education and Child Development. (2019). Transforming tasks: Designing tasks where students do the thinking [Chart]. Retrieved from https://acleadersresource.sa.edu.au/features/transforming-tasks/Transforming_tasks_overview_chart.pdf

Hattie, J. A. C. (2012). *Visible learning for teachers. Maximizing impact on learning.* New York: Routledge.

Hattie, J. (2019a, June). *Visible Learning™ 250+ influences on student achievement.* Retrieved from https://us.corwin.com/sites/default/files/250_influences_chart_june_2019.pdf

Hattie, J. (2019b, July). *Visible Learning™ Metax Influence glossary.* Retrieved from https://www.visiblelearningmetax.com/content/influence_glossary.pdf

Hattie, J., & Timperley, H. (2007). The power of feedback. *Review of Educational Research, 77* (1), 81–112. doi:10.3102/003465430298487

Hill, H. C. (2017). The Coleman Report, 50 years on: What do we know about the role of schools in academic inequality? *Annals of the American Academy of Political and Social Science, 674,* 9–26. doi:10.1177/0002716217727510

Hord, S. M. (2004). Professional learning communities: An overview. In S. M. Hord (Ed.), *Learning together, leading together: Changing schools through professional learning communities* (pp. 5–14). New York: Teachers College Press.

Huang, C. (2016). Achievement goals and self-efficacy: A meta-analysis. *Educational Research Review, 19,* 119–137. doi:10.1016/j.edurev.2016.07.002

Johnson, D., & Johnson, R. (1990). Cooperative learning and achievement. In S. Sharan (Ed.), *Cooperative learning: Theory and research* (pp. 23–37). New York: Praeger.

Johnson, D. W., & Johnson, R. T. (2009). An educational psychology success story: Social interdependence theory and cooperative learning. *Educational Researcher, 38*(5), 365–379. doi:10.3102/0013189X09339057

Johnson, D. W., Johnson, R., & Holubec, E. (2013). *Cooperation in the classroom* (9th ed.). Edina, MN: Interaction Book Company.

Kagan, S. (1994). *Cooperative learning.* San Clemente, CA: Resources for Teachers.

Kapur, M. (2016). Examining productive failure, productive success, unproductive failure, and unproductive success in learning. *Educational Psychologist, 51*(2), 289–299. doi:10.1080/00461520.2016.1155457

Kozlowski, S. W. J., & Ilgen, D. R. (2006). Enhancing the effectiveness of work groups and teams. *Psychological Science in the Public Interest, 7*(3), 77–124. doi:10.1111/j.1529-1006.2006.00030.x

Krashen, S. D. (1987). *Principles and practice in second language acquisition.* Upper Saddle River, NJ: Prentice Hall.

Lazarus, R. S. (1991). *Emotion and adaptation.* New York: Oxford University Press.

Leonard, J. (2001). How group composition influenced the achievement of sixth-grade mathematics students. *Mathematical Thinking and Learning, 3,* 175–200. doi:10.1080/10986065.2001.9679972

Levy, I., Kaplan, A., & Patrick, H. (2000, April). *Early adolescents' achievement goals, inter-group processes, and attitudes towards collaboration.* Paper presented at the annual meeting of the American Educational Research Association, New Orleans, LA.

Lockl, K., & Schneider, W. (2006). Precursors of metamemory in young children: The role of theory of mind and metacognitive vocabulary. *Metacognition and Learning, 1*(1), 15–31. doi:10.1007/s11409-006-6585-9

Lou, Y., Abrami, P. C., Spence, J. C., Poulsen, C., Chambers, B., & d'Appollonia, S. (1996). Within-class grouping: A meta-analysis. *Review of Educational Research, 66,* 423–458. doi:10.3102/00346543066004423

Marzano, R. J. (2010/2011, December–January). When students track their progress. *Educational Leadership, 67*(4), 86–87.

Mason, B., & Thomas, S. (2008). *A million penguins research report.* Retrieved from https://www.researchgate.net/publication/228465833_A_million_penguins_research_report/link/0c9605225a8c559231000000/download

Medina, J. (2008). *Brain rules: 12 principles for surviving and thriving at work, home, and school*. Seattle, WA: Pear Press.

Meijnen, G. W., & Guldemond, H. (2002). Grouping in primary schools and reference processes. *Educational Research and Evaluation, 8*(3), 229–248. doi:10.1076/edre.8.3.229.3857

Moon, J. (2004). *A handbook of reflective and experiential learning: Theory and practice*. London: Routledge Falmer.

NGSS Lead States. (2013). *Next generation science standards: For states, by states*. Washington, DC: National Academies Press.

Nurenberg, D. (2016). Honoring all learners: The case for embedded honors in heterogeneous English language arts classrooms. *English Education, 49*(1), 63–98.

Nuthall, G. (2007). *The hidden lives of learners*. Wellington, New Zealand: NZCER Press.

Oakes, J. (2005). *Keeping track: How schools structure inequality* (2nd ed.). New Haven, CT: Yale University Press.

Ogle, D. M. (1986). K-W-L: A teaching model that develops active reading of expository text. *The Reading Teacher, 39,* 564–570. Retrieved from https://www.jstor.org/stable/20199156

Perner, J. (1991). *Understanding the representational mind*. Cambridge, MA: MIT Press/Bradford Books.

Pianta, R. C., & Hamre, B. K. (2009). Conceptualization, measurement, and improvement of classroom processes: Standardized observation can leverage capacity. *Educational Researcher, 38,* 109–119. doi:10.1207/s15326985ep3902_1

Pianta, R. C., Hamre, B. K., Hayes, N., Mintz, S., & LaParo, K. M. (2011). *Classroom assessment scoring system: Secondary (CLASS-S)*. Charlottesville: University of Virginia.

Plucker, J. A., Beghetto, R. A., & Dow, G. T. (2004). Why isn't creativity more important to educational psychologists? Potentials, pitfalls, and future directions in creativity research. *Educational Psychologist, 39*(2), 83–96. doi:10.1207/s15326985ep3902_1

Poupore, G. (2013). Task motivation in process: A complex systems perspective. *Canadian Modern Language Review, 69*(1), 91–116. doi:10.3138/cmlr.1139

Roberson, B., & Franchini, B. (2014). Effective task design for the TBL classroom. *Journal on Excellence in College Teaching, 25*(3&4), 275–302.

Roseth, C. J., Johnson, D. W., & Johnson, R. T. (2008). Promoting early adolescents' achievement and peer relationships: The effects of cooperative, competitive, and individualistic goal structures. *Psychological Bulletin, 134*(2), 223–246. doi:10.1037/0033-2909.134.2.223

Schlechty, P. C. (2011). *Engaging students: The next level of working on the work*. San Francisco: Jossey-Bass.

Schön, D. A. (1983). *The reflective practitioner: How professionals think in action*. New York: Basic Books.

Shiota, M. N., Keltner, D., & Mossman, A. (2007). The nature of awe: Elicitors, appraisals, and effects on self-concept. *Cognition and Emotion, 21*(5), 944–963. doi:10.1080/02699930600923668

Silvia, P. J. (2010). Confusion and interest: The role of knowledge emotions in aesthetic experience. *Psychology of Aesthetics, Creativity, and the Arts, 4*(2), 75–80.

Silvia, P. (2020). Knowledge emotions: Feelings that foster learning, exploring, and reflecting. In R. Biswas-Diener & E. Diener (Eds.), *NOBA textbook series: Psychology*. Retrieved from http://noba.to/f7rvqp54

Simmons, J. (2003). Responders are taught, not born. *Journal of Adolescent and Adult Literacy, 46*(8), 684–693.

Steiner, I. D. (1972). *Group processes and productivity*. New York: Academic Press.

Sturm, J. M., & Nelson, N. W. (1997). Formal classroom lessons: New perspectives on a familiar discourse event. *Language, Speech, and Hearing Services in Schools, 28*(3), 255–273. doi:10.1044 /0161-1461.2803.255

Surowiecki, J. (2005). *The wisdom of crowds.* Norwell, MA: Anchor.

Tereshchenko, A., Francis, B., Archer, L., Hodgen, J., Mazenod, A., Taylor, B., . . . & Pepper, D. (2019). Learners' attitudes to mixed-attainment grouping: Examining the views of students of high, middle and low attainment. *Research Papers in Education, 34*(4), 425–444. doi:10.1080/02671522.2018.1452962

Tyng, C. M., Amin, H. U., Saad, M., & Malik, A. S. (2017). The influences of emotion on learning and memory. *Frontiers in Psychology, 8,* 1454. doi:10.3389/fpsyg.2017.01454

Vanderbilt, T. (2009). *Traffic: Why we drive the way we do (and what it says about us).* New York: Alfred A. Knopf.

Webb, N. (1997). *Criteria for alignment of expectations and assessments in mathematics and science education.* Washington, DC: Council of Chief State School Officers.

Webb, N., & Mastergeorge, A. (2003). Promoting effective helping in peer-directed groups. *International Journal of Educational Research, 39,* 73–97. doi:10.1016/S0883-0355(03)00074-0

Webb, N. M., Nemer, K. M., & Ing, M. (2006). Small-group reflections: Parallels between teacher discourse and student behavior in peer-directed groups. *Journal of the Learning Sciences, 15*(1), 63–119. doi:10.1207/s15327809jls1501_8

Wilkinson, I. A. G., & Nelson, K. (2013). Role of discussion in reading comprehension. In J. Hattie & E. Anderman (Eds.), *International guide to student achievement* (pp. 299–302). New York: Routledge.

Index

The letter *f* following a page number denotes a figure.

About the Authors

 **Douglas Fisher** is a professor of educational leadership at San Diego State University and a teacher leader at Health Sciences High & Middle College. He is a member of the California Reading Hall of Fame and is the recipient of a Celebrate Literacy Award from the International Reading Association, the Farmer Award for Excellence in Writing from the National Council of Teachers of English, and the Christa McAuliffe Award for Excellence in Teacher Education from the American Association of State Colleges and Universities. Fisher has published numerous articles on improving student achievement, and his books include *The Purposeful Classroom*, *Building Equity*, and *Intentional and Targeted Teaching*. He can be reached at dfisher@sdsu.edu.

 **Nancy Frey** is a professor of educational leadership at San Diego State University and a teacher leader at Health Sciences High & Middle College. Before joining the university faculty, Frey was a special education teacher in the Broward County (Florida) Public Schools, where she taught students at the elementary and middle school levels. She later worked for the Florida Department of Education on a statewide project for supporting students with disabilities in a general education curriculum. Frey is a recipient of the Christa McAuliffe Award for Excellence in Teacher Education from the American Association of

State Colleges and Universities and the Early Career Award from the Literacy Research Association. Her research interests include reading and literacy, assessment, intervention, and curriculum design. She has published many articles and books on literacy and instruction, including *Better Learning Through Structured Teaching, How to Reach the Hard to Teach,* and *All Learning Is Social and Emotional.* She can be reached at nfrey@sdsu.edu.

 **John Almarode** is an associate professor of education and the Executive Director of Teaching and Learning in the College of Education at James Madison University. Almarode began his career in Augusta County, Virginia, teaching high school mathematics and science. Now, he works with preservice teachers and devotes time to collaborating with in-service teachers in classrooms and schools across the globe. Almarode and his colleagues have presented their work to the U.S. Congress, the U.S. Department of Education, and the White House Office of Science and Technology Policy. He has authored multiple articles, reports, book chapters, and more than a dozen books on effective teaching and learning in today's schools and classrooms. He can be reached at almarojt@jmu.edu.

Related ASCD Resources: Learning in Community

At the time of publication, the following resources were available (ASCD stock numbers in parentheses):

All Learning Is Social and Emotional: Helping Students Develop Essential Skills for the Classroom and Beyond by Nancy Frey, Douglas Fisher, and Dominique Smith (#119033)

Better Learning Through Structured Teaching: A Framework for the Gradual Release of Responsibility (2nd edition) by Douglas Fisher and Nancy Frey (#113006)

Grading and Group Work: How do I assess individual learning when students work together? (ASCD Arias) by Susan M. Brookhart (#SF113073)

Questioning for Classroom Discussion: Purposeful Speaking, Engaged Listening, Deep Thinking by Jackie Acree Walsh and Beth Dankert Sattes (#115012)

Teaching to Empower: Taking Action to Foster Student Agency, Self-Confidence, and Collaboration by Debbie Zacarian and Michael Silverstone (#120006)

For up-to-date information about ASCD resources, go to www.ascd.org. You can search the complete archives of *Educational Leadership* at www.ascd.org/el.

ASCD myTeachSource®
Download resources from a professional learning platform with hundreds of research-based best practices and tools for your classroom at http://myteachsource.ascd.org/

For more information, send an e-mail to member@ascd.org; call 1-800-933-2723 or 703-578-9600; send a fax to 703-575-5400; or write to Information Services, ASCD, 1703 N. Beauregard St., Alexandria, VA 22311-1714 USA.

WHOLE CHILD
TENETS

1 HEALTHY
Each student enters school healthy and learns about and practices a healthy lifestyle.

2 SAFE
Each student learns in an environment that is physically and emotionally safe for students and adults.

3 ENGAGED
Each student is actively engaged in learning and is connected to the school and broader community.

4 SUPPORTED
Each student has access to personalized learning and is supported by qualified, caring adults.

5 CHALLENGED
Each student is challenged academically and prepared for success in college or further study and for employment and participation in a global environment.

THE WHOLE CHILD

The ASCD Whole Child approach is an effort to transition from a focus on narrowly defined academic achievement to one that promotes the long-term development and success of all children. Through this approach, ASCD supports educators, families, community members, and policymakers as they move from a vision about educating the whole child to sustainable, collaborative actions.

Student Learning Communities relates to the **healthy**, **safe**, **engaged**, **supported**, and **challenged** tenets.

For more about the ASCD Whole Child approach, visit **www. ascd.org/wholechild.**

Become an ASCD member today!
Go to www.ascd.org/joinascd
or call toll-free: 800-933-ASCD (2723)

LEARN. TEACH. LEAD.